DONOSO CORTES

Cassandra of the Age

DONOSO CORTES

Cassandra of the Age

R. A. Herrera

With a Foreword by
Frederick D. Wilhelmsen

WILLIAM B. EERDMANS PUBLISHING COMPANY
GRAND RAPIDS, MICHIGAN / CAMBRIDGE, U.K.

© 1995 Wm. B. Eerdmans Publishing Co.
255 Jefferson Ave. S.E., Grand Rapids, Michigan 49503 /
P. O. Box 163, Cambridge CB3 9PU U.K.

Printed in the United States of America

00 99 98 97 96 95   7 6 5 4 3 2 1

Library of Congress Cataloging-in-Publication Data

Herrera, Robert A.
Donoso Cortés: Cassandra of the age / R. A. Herrera.
p.   cm.
Includes bibliographical references and index.
ISBN 0-8028-0874-3 (alk. paper)
1. Donoso Cortés, Juan, marqués de Valdegamas, 1809-1853 — Political and social
views. 2. Donoso Cortés, Juan, marqués de Valdegamas, 1809-1853 — Religion.
3. Spain — Politics and government — 1833-1868. 4. Diplomats — Spain —
Biography. 5. Authors, Spanish — 19th century — Biography.
6. Intellectuals — Spain — Biography.   I. Title.
DP202.D6H47   1995
946′.072′092 — dc20
[B]   95-34280
CIP

The author gratefully acknowledges a grant made by The Wilbur Foundation during the
writing of this book.

To Deborah

Contents

Foreword

Don Juan Donoso Cortés is one of those rare figures whom academicians find difficult to slot into any conventional category. To some, Donoso is little more than a diplomat and politician turned journalist. To others, Donoso is altogether a theologian, albeit one with dubious credentials. Some see him as a prophet. To still others, Donoso is a full-fledged political philosopher. A few, such as the illustrious Spanish jurist Alvaro d'Ors, might call him a political theologian. Granting some validity to all of these definitions, I must say that my own judgment leans in the direction of this last one: that Donoso is a political theologian. The eminent Spanish figure — diplomat, journalist, politician, philosopher, theologian, or whatever else one might call him — complicates the life of anyone attempting to understand him because he constantly amended his own thought, changing it as he sloughed off earlier formulations and added new insights to his vision of existence.

His short life was mercurial; and just as mercury is impossible to fix, due to its essential fluidity, the definitive word on the man seems to escape the scope of definition. Considered by Professor Vincent McNamara to have been a liberal, he was one — but he abandoned that standard some few years before his death. Treated by some German scholars as an apologist for dictatorship, Donoso was one

— but only for a moment, which swiftly passed as he moved to a deeper understanding of the Catholic political tradition. Interpreted by others as a traditionalist and crypto-Carlist, he was one — but only when death stared him in the face. Professor Federico Suárez understands him as a man whose thought can be divided into four or five essential moments; and there are, indeed, "moments" in Donoso's history. But the division itself, intelligently forged and hammered into unity by the Spanish historian, tends to melt into the Heraclitean hurry marking the life of a man who never stopped, who knew no repose; of a contemplative spirit destined to a life of action; of a suave diplomat who juggled treaties and alliances, but who wore a hair shirt under all his finery.

No contemporary student of Don Juan Donoso Cortés has captured what I have called here the fluidity of his life with greater sympathy and profundity than the author of this book, Professor R. A. Herrera. Dr. Herrera, a distinguished student of mysticism in its Jewish, Christian, and Islamic dimensions, a scholar of the thought of St. Anselm, has found in Donoso a worthy subject of his many talents. If Suárez *sees* Donoso (and sight fixes reality, freezing it in frames), then Herrera *feels* the man as he moves from posture to position, from extravagant polemics to profound meditations on the meaning of humanity's existence in history. To read this book is to enter into the motley and the kaleidoscope of early nineteenth-century Europe and to sense Donoso's role from within its very moving complexity.

The mark of an artist is to forge into aesthetic unity the materials with which he works. R. A. Herrera's style in this book parallels the haste with which Donoso lived his short life. From within, we palpate Don Juan's early liberal enthusiasm, its rapid tempering in the waters of a Spanish politics where liberalism seemed always to diminish or jeopardize the Catholic essence of Spain, which Donoso loved from his earliest years in the harsh country of his birth, Extremadura, land of the conquistadors. We experience (in my case, with exasperation) the young man's lyrical and romantic loyalty to the Queen Regent despite the crown's having been captured by anticlerical forces and by military adventurers hostile to the religion of the nation, Donoso's own religion. We are with the young diplomat in Paris, where he was more or less at home, and in Berlin, where he was not at home at all. We follow him through the salons of Paris, and we descend into the hell of the slums of that city, where the Spaniard gave away his money and even his garments to the poor, always disguising his charity under the facade of a sophisticated elegance and a polished exterior which seemed to mock the world in which he perforce lived.

The writings of Donoso as parliamentarian and orator, theoretician and prophet, are presented by Dr. Herrera always within the historical moment which gave them birth. With the possible exception of his great *Catolicismo, Liberalismo, Socialismo,* all of Donoso's works were ad hoc responses, whether written or delivered as spoken addresses, to immediate political crises. Even his letter answering the liberal Duke de Broglie, a letter which is a nugget of political philosophy, was thought through and executed in the context of a controversy, a battle between two minds. His passionate appeal to the queen to divest herself of her jewels in the service of the poor of Spain was a quixotic foreshadowing of the social encyclicals of Leo XIII and Pius XI.

His most original theory is the law of unity and variety in all being as adumbrating the inner life of the Holy Trinity. "In that inaccessible Tabernacle," writes Donoso, "where there is worked perpetually the prodigy of all prodigies and the Mystery of all Mysteries . . . , there is the God of Catholicism: One and Triune — unity expanding itself and engendering an eternal variety, as well as variety condensing itself and resolving itself onto an eternal unity." From this blaze of trinitarian mystery, Donoso built his political philosophy, which saw a decent social and political order as one synthesizing a unity of power with a variety of free and autonomous institutions, and placing in the prime position the family, itself an analogue of the Holy Trinity.

His adoption of St. Augustine's *credo ut intelligam* ("I believe in order that I might understand") makes of Donoso — in some sense, at least — a latter-day Augustinian theologian of political existence. The doctrine itself, however, was pressured into being as Donoso contemplated with horror the effects of the French Revolution and its devastation of the older harmony marking Catholic civilization. His prophetic vision of Russia advancing as a great bear out of the East to castigate a Europe sickened in sin was an apocalyptic message, but it came as a conclusion drawn by a working diplomat whom some have compared to St. Augustine. Donoso, living in a Europe still glittering with the pomp and splendor of a past age, saw — and only he saw — what was to come. He predicted the future of Communism with greater accuracy than did its founders, Marx and Engels.

In my opinion, Don Juan Donoso Cortés was the greatest of all of the theoreticians of the Counter-Revolution, even though none of his intuitions ever fructified into a complete theory. His insistence on the absolute, not relative, superiority of Catholic civilization over both classical antiquity and the Western world ushered into history by the Protestant revolt needed a Christopher Dawson to footnote it. His philosophical insistence on the unicity of power and its limitations by "the hierarchies" needed an Alvaro d'Ors for its articulation in terms of the questioning nature of power and the answering nature of authority. His law of variety and unity in all being needed the earlier Thomistic analogy of proper proportionality for its full metaphysical expression. A Chesterton before Chesterton in his amazing sense of paradox ("Variety *is* unity, and unity *is* variety"), and a Belloc before Belloc ("Europe is the Faith, and the Faith is Europe"), Donoso centered in himself a tradition already in existence and a flowering thereof yet to come.

Dr. Herrera does not halt to explore in detail any of Don Juan's theories, either those churned into being and then discarded or those grown to maturity in a life cut short by a ghastly disease. Our author simply follows his subject through time. Herrera's very prose mirrors the nervous energy of this unpredictable genius who became, in the end, the one man in all of Europe who was most hated by the Left — especially the Catholic Left — with a hatred that was, according to Carl Schmitt, almost metaphysical in its intensity. Dr. Herrera has written a book which is an intellectual history. This intellectual history weaves, as would a boat in troubled waters, through the sea of half a century, the first part of the nineteenth, an era which Donoso loathed and which has made our own world to be what it is: wounded and afraid.

Frederick D. Wilhelmsen
Professor of Philosophy and Politics
University of Dallas, Irving, Texas

Preface

We live in the age of Caliban. It is not necessary to read Nietzsche, Spengler, or Ortega to realize that the "last man" — "mass man," the "trousered ape" — has come into his own. A case can be made that the new barbarian has been generated by the laborious and painful process by which Western man was surgically detached from his past and his God. This horizontal and vertical separation has produced a humanity without historical perspective and tradition, unconcerned about the fragility of civilization, with close ties to the irrational and the perverse. Like Kafka's Gregor Samsa, contemporary man is alienated, willing to barter his humanity to escape an intolerable situation. Like Gregor, we distinctly hear the gnashing of teeth above the clatter of the silverware.

The seeds of this malaise were planted over two centuries ago, at the center of a great expanse of leveling which subverted European monarchy. Carl Schmitt was perhaps naive in pinpointing three blows as having injured the roots of Europe: the civil conflicts of 1848, the First World War, and what he called (in a lecture given in Madrid on May 31, 1944) "the present civil war which extends throughout the planet."[1] But he was hardly naive when he noted that Donoso Cortés's name

1. Carl Schmitt, *Interpretación Europea de Donoso Cortés* (Madrid: Rialp, 1963), p. 27.

resounds among the echoes of catastrophe only to lapse into silence when these moments of panic have passed. A few decades ago, Luis Araquistáin observed that each resuscitation of interest in Donoso has coincided with the establishment of a dictatorship.[2] Spanish criticism has been ambivalent. Múñoz Alonso has kind words for Donoso, though he ranks Jaime Balmes as a "philosopher" and Donoso as a mere "thinker."[3] However, Federico Suárez, the doyen of Donoso studies, ranks him as possibly the greatest Spanish mind of the past three centuries; a familiarity with Donoso's work is, he says, invaluable for the proper understanding of European history in the aftermath of the French Revolution.[4]

Donoso has been little studied in the United States. In the middle of the nineteenth century, Orestes Brownson, impressed by his eloquence, wrote two incisive studies.[5] In the present century, Peter Viereck has made perceptive observations concerning Donoso in two idiosyncratic volumes; in Viereck's judgment, Donoso was "in some ways . . . the subtlest intellect in the entire history of conservatism."[6] Professor John Graham has authored a careful and informative volume,[7] and Frederick D. Wilhelmsen an insightful study,[8] each of which, in its own way, has yet to be surpassed.

The early studies by Edmund Schramm[9] and Dietmar West-

2. Luis Araquistáin, "Donoso Cortés y su resonancia en Europa," *Cuadernos* 3 (September-December 1953): 12.

3. Múñoz Alonso, *Letteratura e Filosofía di Spagna* (Bari: Editoriale Universitaria, 1969), pp. 84-91, 224.

4. Federico Suárez Verdeguer, *Introducción a Donoso Cortés* (Madrid: Rialp, 1964), pp. 7, 264.

5. Orestes Brownson, "Union of Church and State," *Catholic World* (April 1867); "Rights and Duties," *Brownson's Review* (October 1852).

6. Peter Viereck, *Conservatism: From John Adams to Churchill* (Princeton: D. Van Nostrand, 1956), p. 12. See also his *Conservatism Revisited* (New York: Charles Scribner's Sons, 1950).

7. John T. Graham, *Donoso Cortés: Utopian Romanticist and Political Realist* (Columbia: University of Missouri Press, 1974), p. 14.

8. Frederick D. Wilhelmsen, "Donoso Cortés and the Problem of Political Power," *Intercollegiate Review* (January-February 1967).

9. Edmund Schramm, *Donoso Cortés, su Vida y su Pensamiento*, trans. Ramón de la Serna (Madrid: Espasa-Calpe, 1936).

emeyer[10] are still of great value. Spanish scholarship, though at times marred by intramural partisanship, includes such competent studies as those of Calvo Serer, Ceñal, Elías de Tejada, and Galindo.[11] The transpyrenean scholarship of the past half century contains interesting tangential studies, notably those of Erich Przywara, Bela Menczer, and Karl Löwith.[12] South American scholarship takes up the task in the work of Sánchez Abelenda.[13] New translations also seem to augur a renewed interest.

It would be a well-nigh impossible task to review the harsh attacks which have been launched against Donoso or to explain the intense hatred this kind and charitable man has generated. Along with Pius IX and the French traditionalists, he has been castigated as an enemy of the "Greek spirit," a man aspiring to rekindle the fires of the Inquisition, an atavistic regression to the Dark Ages, and worse. A few decades ago, Friedrich Heer added a contemporary twist, interpreting Donoso's angst as a compound of Spanish Manichaean elements and suppressed homosexual tendencies.[14]

In spite of these attacks, Juan Donoso Cortés is probably one of the most acute, if idiosyncratic, diagnosticians of the age. Like Pius IX, he flirted with liberalism only to react violently against it. The present was dark and growing darker; the future was terrifying. It was, indeed, Schmitt who suggested that Donoso was a Cassandra figure — someone whose predictions, while repeatedly rejected, continually increase in value.[15] Donoso's prophetic stance, coupled with his apocalyptic style and notable lack of systematization, makes it difficult, if not impossible, to fit him into an appropriate slot. Is

10. Dietmar Westemeyer, *Donoso Cortés, hombre de Estado y Teólogo,* trans. J. S. Mazpule (Madrid: Editora Nacional, 1957).

11. For an extensive bibliography, see *Obras Completas de Don Juan Donoso Cortés,* vol. 1, ed. Carlos Valverde, S.J. (Madrid: BAC, 1970), pp. 157-66.

12. See note 11.

13. Raul Sánchez Abelenda, *La teoría del poder en el pensamiento político de Juan Donoso Cortés* (Buenos Aires: EUDBA, 1969).

14. Friedrich Heer, *Europe: Mother of Revolutions,* trans. C. Kessler and J. Adcock (New York: Praeger, 1972), p. 259.

15. Schmitt, pp. 29-31.

he a philosopher, a theologian, a thinker, a "phantasticus" in the manner of Ramon Llull, a psychopathological monstrosity, or a mere eccentric? This challenge to the schematizing proclivities of the academic mind may account in part for the relative obscurity to which he has been consigned, in comparison to figures of equal or less historical importance.

The most profound reason for the massive hostility Donoso has inspired in the fourteen decades since his death is probably his penchant for putting modernity's myths, beliefs, and institutions on the block. Donoso is a gauntlet thrown against the "good things" of our public orthodoxy. If he happens to be correct, even in part, then many of our contemporaries — indeed, people of all generations dating from the French Revolution — are convicted of living a lie, their senses dulled by illusion and chatter. Is it possible that mankind is blundering into a totalitarianism disguised as a humanism based on the democratic principle of the greatest good for the greatest number?

Donoso's influence on the nineteenth century was an exceptional feat for a Spanish journalist, politician, and diplomat bound to a decadent monarchy and living in a society divided by war, ideology, and class. Many of his works were translated into German, French, and Italian. He was cited with approval by Schelling, Metternich, Ranke, Frederick William IV, and others. Donoso was able to transcend the Byzantine intrigues of the Spanish court, which he served as a gray eminence, to become a major figure in the wider world of European diplomacy. But he was not able to detach his thought from its geographical point of departure, marked as it is by exaggeration, a definite pragmatic orientation, and a taste for the elegantly dramatic. He was engaged in a struggle to the death with ideologies which took on terrifying, grotesque, and enfleshed forms. This was not a matter of merely speculative web-spinning. What was at stake for real life probably accounts for his controversial ferocity and pessimism, for the flashes of light found within his labored argumentation. Tediously apocalyptic as it can at times be, his thought usually stays within the limits of rationality. His is never empty fustian. The historical perch he occupied gave Donoso a unique view of the vicissitudes of European civilization.

As a young man, Donoso was captivated by the French Enlightenment — a fascination furthered under the tutelage of Manuel José Quintana. His studies at Salamanca and Seville served to strengthen his liberalism, as did the pervasive romanticism of the age. His readings were heavily tilted toward French authors; his early political activity gravitated toward the moderate liberalism of the coterie surrounding María Cristina. This orientation is reflected in the *Lecciones de derecho político* (1836-1837) where the influence of Destutt-Tracy and Condillac is obvious. However, a turn away from liberalism is already evidenced in these lectures, a turn that became more pronounced as Donoso entered into the arena of Spanish intellectual and political life.

The death of his brother Pedro in 1847 and the "year of revolutions" (1848) completed Donoso's *metanoia*. The enemy was now revolution. Europe was in the grip of a revolutionary fever that showed little sign of diminishing and that generated a burgeoning neopaganism. Donoso viewed this neopaganism as the malevolent double of Christianity, a parody drawing its considerable strength from its source. The state begins to recover the terrible omnipotence it once possessed. Reason is enthroned as the national god. Limit and boundary vanish with the enfeeblement of the Church and the waning of religious belief. Force becomes the only ruling principle. But revolution is also the instrument of a higher power (his pages on the French monarchy are canny), and it flows along the grooves determined by Providence. He rejects popular wisdom to affirm that revolution is caused by the exacerbated desires of masses exploited by demagogues. Yet Donoso was not blind to the existence of rank injustice. In 1851, in a magnificent though futile gesture, he directed an appeal to the Queen Mother stressing how urgently social reform was needed, if only to avert a universal insurrection.

Once disenchanted with the thought of such French philosophers as Destutt-Tracy and Condillac, he began to launch a bitter attack against a rationalism he believed to have spawned the most noxious of philosophies and ideologies — those having infected the masses, in a manner similar to that of "English opium," with their presupposition of the autonomy of reason and their envisioning of the possibility of human perfectibility, their utopian pretense of transforming this vale of tears into a garden of delights. Donoso came to reject the romantic ideal of everlasting discussion, and predicted the advent of a debased, chattering mass, a humanity leveled beyond redemption.

Philosophy cannot ground society. Donoso postulates philosophy as having been concocted by a reason rebelling against God and consequently functioning out of its proper relation to the truth. Man's Promethean stance conflicts with the legitimate sovereignty of God and truth. Prometheus's gift entails human suffering. Hesiod, Aeschylus, and Plato state as much. Donoso discovers a "secret affinity" between human reason and the absurd, a "secret repugnance" between reason and truth. Only religion can provide, and has provided, society with a solid foundation, since only religion is not subject to the fluctuations of reason. Donoso therefore strongly commends the often decried doctrinal intolerance of the Church. It is the Church, and only the Church, that has saved the world from chaos, by placing those truths which ground the social, political, and domestic orders beyond the corrosive influence of discussion.

Overwhelmed by the contradictions of a modernity which rejects dogma and entrusts the weightiest questions to the determination of public assemblies and the press, Donoso saw the result as global catastrophe. Truth and error are conflated; society enters into a realm of shadows, deliberate deception, and pervasive illusion. Religion — the only hope for humanity — has been discarded. This hierarchical upset is reflected in the corruption of society at large. It should come as no surprise that the media have come to be the most respected authority. Their very essence is illusion; they appear to be everything they are not and are nothing they appear to be.

Rationalism is the seedbed of both liberalism (of the kind associated with constitutional monarchy and the rule of the bourgeoisie) and socialism (a meld of egalitarianism and romanticism). Donoso believed rationalism to be endemically feeble. It would, ineluctably, lead to the desacralization of society and to a regression to paganism. At first he was seduced by the vision of rule by the "natural aristocracies" and the "principle of intelligence," but he soon became disenchanted and came to view this way of thinking as an unsatisfactory halfway house doomed to extinction. He saw the obsession with discussion as limiting the scope of liberalism to the political domain and as leading to the paralysis of concrete action.

Incapable of grandeur or heroism, liberalism is in Donoso's eyes the breeding ground of socialism, which takes the liberal's common rationalist credo to its ultimate conclusions. Both liberalism and socialism ignore the organic character of society, its historical building up through sedimentation, and any connection between past and future. While liberalism proposes laissez-faireism (defined by Donoso as pagan egotism without the virility of pagan hatred), socialism glories in the vaguest and most abstract of solidarities — that of simply being human — while eschewing the familial, religious, and professional associations which provide the necessary ground and support of all human solidarity.

Donoso viewed socialism as the polar opposite of Christianity. Socialism, he said, rejects the Christian notion of grace and replaces it with absolute autonomy; it trades in revelation for the omnipotence of reason, Divine Providence for the sovereignty of mankind. Socialism is rationalistic, democratic, and atheistic. Donoso did harbor a grudging admiration for socialists, inasmuch as they propose radical solutions and penetrate to the depths of things. Though he agreed with de Maistre in considering them demonic, he had to concede that unlike the liberals, who just floated on the surface, the socialists possessed a "theology," a system of thought, as well as their own "theologians."

From the beginning and throughout many vicissitudes, Donoso repeatedly affirmed that the religious domain is the foundation of all other domains. It followed, therefore, that every social or political aberration must be reducible to a religious aberration — in other words, a heresy. The plethora of modern "errors" was the outcome of two principal heresies: the denial of sin and the denial of Providence. Liberalism ignored the existence of sin and its chilling effects. Socialism denied that sin exists, affirming that human nature is good and that evil is generated by institutions. Socialism, in proclaiming mankind's "immaculate conception," was simply drawing out the ultimate consequences of the pantheism espoused by liberalism and reflected in the hubris of the masses aspiring to universal domination.

A cataclysm was approaching. All events, all ideas, were converging to produce it. Defense strategies were doomed since liberalism and socialism had destroyed the very concept of authority. The nations had become ungovernable. Donoso resembles Calhoun in his conviction that unlimited freedom and equality are noxious, that government becomes despotic and absolute to the extent that the people become debased and corrupt. He maintains that only two kinds of repression are possible: inner (religious) and outer (political). As religion loses its hold on the masses, political repression will necessarily keep increasing to the point of generating a monstrous tyranny. This tyranny will be nurtured by those very acts of religious and moral emancipation which are the boast of modernity — acts which grow all the more oppressive as the last vestiges of Christianity are excised from society. The possibility of resistance has been weakened by the corrosive effect of the media, the destruction of patriotism, and apoplectic centralization. The coming tyranny will be "gigantesco, colosal, inmenso!"

Donoso believed that only a massive countermovement of Christian renewal could avert this catastrophe, that only a recovery of the notions of command and obedience, order and liberty, rule and limit, could halt the decline. One suspects that he did not really believe such a renewal was possible. Donoso's last years were spent in anguished expectation, perhaps ameliorated by the belief he shared with Deutero-Isaiah that deliverance would finally come, not from men, but from God, who would someday usher in the world to come.[16] Nonetheless, delaying actions were not only possible but

16. See D. S. Russell, *The Method and Message of Jewish Apocalyptic* (Philadelphia: Westminster, 1964), pp. 265-67.

imperative. Donoso's advocacy of dictatorship and his much debated "decisionism" can be understood only in this light.

To the contemporary eye, Donoso's speculations may seem archaic and pessimistic to an extreme, analogous to Goya's black sketches. But if he was right in characterizing his epoch as the absurd competing with the grotesque, and in entertaining little hope on a purely natural level, this negative realism is balanced by a larger view in which evil is ultimately defeated by means of direct divine intervention. Donoso was influenced by many — above all, especially in his later years, by St. Augustine.[17] He appropriated Augustine's majestic themes and incorporated them into his thought, in typically arbitrary fashion. Donoso admitted to being a divided man, with one foot in the world and the other in the cloister. Few men have had the agonizing task of reconciling such glaring opposites: severity with meekness, lordliness with tact, sensuality with spirituality, pride with humility. Donoso died as he had lived, in poverty of spirit amidst the splendors of the Spanish Embassy in Paris.

17. See my "The Great in the Small: Donoso Cortés' Variation on a Theme from the *Civitas Dei*," *Augustiniana* (1988), fas. 1-4, pp. 140-47.

CHAPTER ONE

Introduction: Mirror of an Age

Donoso's reactions to the vicissitudes of his epoch can reasonably be viewed as exaggerated, if not pathological. At times he himself viewed them that way. But his reactions tend to appear even beyond the bizarre to enthusiasts of the French Revolution and its sequelae. For example, Heer notes Donoso's "abysmal pessimism" and the proclivity he shared with Bonald and de Maistre to "trample their opponents underfoot by any available means."[1] He includes Donoso, with Pius IX and the Roman Curia, among the enemies of the Greek free spirit. Yet Heer lists, in his interesting but diffuse account, a catalogue of monstrosities that would have justified Donoso or any other tradition-minded person in taking a critical look at this period and advocating draconian measures. This justification is corroborated by other works, such as those of James Billington,[2] J. B. Bury,[3] and A. L. Guerard,[4] that probe into the

1. Friedrich Heer, *Europe: Mother of Revolutions,* trans. C. Kessler and J. Adcock (New York: Praeger, 1972), pp. 67, 245, 254, 259, and 277.

2. James H. Billington, *Fire in the Minds of Men: Origins of the Revolutionary Faith* (New York: Basic Books, 1980).

3. J. B. Bury, *The Idea of Progress* (New York: Macmillan, 1932), and *A History of Freedom of Thought* (New York: Henry Holt, 1913).

4. A. L. Guerard, *French Civilization in the Nineteenth Century* (New York: Century, 1918).

sources of the revolutionary fervor. Not all of these sources are examples of rigorous scholarship, but they all deserve to be cited at least because of the light they cast on the epoch. Schmitt — who has been criticized for many things, but never for lack of scholarship — covers the ground to some extent and claims that the exotic satanism of the period was "not an incidental paradox but a powerful intellectual principle."[5] Inasmuch as it serves as a backdrop to the "era of revolutions," and consequently to Donoso's perspective, this period requires some exploration.

De Maistre was not alone in believing that the French Revolution was of a satanic character — that it was, in fact, precisely this characteristic which made it a unique phenomenon, a historical *novum*. The period of gestation for this earth-shattering event witnessed the proliferation of sects, factions, and conventicles of enthusiasts. Swedenborgians preached the advent of a new world. William Blake, prodded by his gnostic inclinations, headed a circle of Jacobin sympathizers, preaching a world revolution which would destroy the old order. Extreme Saint-Simonians adopted the cult of the messianic "Great Mother," the "liberator of peoples."[6] Pythagoras became the model for revolutionary intellectuals, and geometric figures were used to symbolize opposition to the Christian, monarchical establishment. Satan and Cain became the favorite symbols of social and sexual liberation: for Baudelaire, Satan was the benefactor of mankind and the patron of the impoverished.[7]

Fundamentally anti-Christian as it was, the generation born of the French Revolution waged a full-scale campaign to appropriate Christian zeal for its own purposes. Humanity aspired to construct a new and superior Christianity which marched to the beat of revolutionary drums. Rousseau prepared the way by launching, in his *Second Discourse,* an assault on the natural law theory, attaching to

---

5. Carl Schmitt, *Political Theology,* trans. G. Schwab (Cambridge: MIT Press, 1985 [1922]), p. 64.

6. Heer, pp. 16, 18-19, and 94.

7. Heer, p. 101; Billington, pp. 99-107.

that assault "a precociously Marxian indictment of private property." With his *Emile* he laid the groundwork for two centuries' worth of educational experimentation, and in his *Social Contract* he made a "clarion call to revolution."[8] His later novels popularized the notions of the naturally good man and the "beautiful soul" and ushered them into the storehouse of common notions, where they in effect displaced the traditional religious universe of discourse.

The revolutionary symbols themselves — the infatuation with nature, the liberty trees (replacing crosses), the dances around the trees and even around the guillotine, the consecration of agricultural implements, and so on[9] — were all parodies of Christian ritual, their theatricality an obvious attempt to supplant liturgical pomp and circumstance. Especially significant was the creation of a new calendar to further their purpose of detaching the new age from its past — a fiction imitated at a later date by a solitary thinker, Nietzsche, who gave his *Der Antichrist* the date of the first day of the year one.[10]

The spirit of the age is reflected in Saint-Simon's *Nouveau Chris-tianisme,* which advocates the constitution of a secular Christianity that will move toward a future golden age. As the past is shelved, the notion of progress begins to acquire mythic proportions. Jean Paul has Christ preaching atheism; Shelley writes *The Necessity of Atheism.* George Sand takes up the cause of the independence of women. Flora Tristan, in *Méphis,* views woman as mediatrix between God and man — an obvious distortion of the traditional role of the Blessed Virgin. Olympia de Gouges drafts a *Declaration of the Rights of Woman,* while Mary Wollstonecraft writes a *Vindication of the Rights of Woman,* taking Edmund Burke to task for his attacks on the French Revolution. (Some years later, her daughter, Mary Shelley, will pen the prescient *Frankenstein.*) Patriarchal society is attacked. Feminism is joined to pacifism and sexual extravagance.

---

8. Peter Fuss, "Rousseau as Critical Theorist: The Argument of the *Second Discourse*" (typescript), p. 2.

9. Billington, pp. 44-53.

10. Friedrich W. Nietzsche, *Der Antichrist* (Berlin: Walter de Gruyter, 1969), p. 252.

La Paix des Deux Mondes, possibly the first pacifist periodical, is founded in Lyon by Eugénie Niboye.[11] Many of these beliefs will later become staples of anarchism.

More important to the theme under consideration is Donoso's bête noire Proudhon, who inverts the Christian theological scenario. To Proudhon's mind, Satan is good and God is evil; God is the enemy of mankind. The task at hand is to substitute man for God. Many German left-Hegelians would be no less insistent on this point.

All of these disparate phenomena can be placed under the heading of Romanticism — a glorification of change and of youth, a reaction against traditional forms and existing social conditions. Romanticism aspired to create a religion which would captivate the modern age as Christianity had captivated the ancient world. It was fashionable to make parallels between this epoch and Rome at the time of its civil wars. Donoso later observed that the pseudo-religion of absolute humanity is a path leading ineluctably to inhuman terror, that every illusory paradise is fated to become a real hell. Nevertheless, these parallels were taken quite seriously and acted upon in the most advanced circles. Alexander Herzen, for example, had no doubt that the revolutionaries of the nineteenth century had a historic role analogous to that of the Christians of the first century. From his perspective, Donoso was nothing more or less than a reactionary apostate.

The fundamental question of politics, ethics, and social theory is of a bare-bones simplicity: "Is man good or evil?" Donoso's answer is that man is both good and evil, but in practice he tilts toward evil. In contrast, the great majority of romantics believed in man's natural goodness. While Enlightenment rationalism taught that man was capable of being educated, the revolutionary ethos went further, teaching that man as "good" or "evil" was just the product of education or a concoction of theological fantasy. But reacting against authority can have unforeseen consequences. Bakunin, the greatest

11. Billington, pp. 483-84.

4

anarchist of the century, became "the theologian of anti-theology and the dictator of anti-dictatorship."[12]

Lessing's *The Education of the Human Race* reflects a further aspect of the revolutionary period. He does not oppose Christianity but, in the tradition of Joachim of Fiore, envisions a third age, the coming reign of human self-realization, which will be the authentic fulfillment of Christian revelation.[13] Fichte, Schelling, and Comte also predict an age of the spirit, a new stage of consciousness, the advent of the secular kingdom of God. Schelling reproduces the Joachimist triad: first, the age of Peter, the apostle of the Father; second, that of Paul, the apostle of the Son; finally, that of John, the apostle of the Spirit. Joachim's three *status* now signify a historical movement in which Catholicism is followed by Protestantism, which is itself crowned by the perfect religion of mankind.[14]

Donoso had substantial reasons for believing that Proudhon was the very incarnation of evil. Proudhon took the revolutionary ethos to its radical conclusion: believing in progress necessitated not believing in God. Proudhon expanded the Joachimist triad into a quaternity. According to this schema, the advance of history springs from certain crises. The first (equality before God) was provoked by Jesus; the second (equality before reason) by the Reformation and Descartes; the third (equality before the law) by the French Revolution. The fourth and final crisis is the one at hand: the equating of man and humanity, so that complete equality can be attained.[15] The greatest obstacle to this goal is God, the source of all absolutism. It follows that if God exists, he should be combated and destroyed.

For Proudhon God is thus equated with evil, and religion is the purveyor of that evil. It is a vampire devouring humanity; it is

12. Carl Schmitt, *Interpretación Europea de Donoso Cortés* (Madrid: Rialp, 1963), p. 92.
13. Karl Löwith, *Meaning in History* (Chicago: University of Chicago Press, 1949), pp. 208-13. See also Henri de Lubac, *Proudhon et le christianisme* (Paris: Editions du Seuil, 1945).
14. Löwith, p. 210.
15. Löwith, pp. 63-65.

something hostile to human nature. God is the ghost of our conscience, "anti-civilisateur, anti-liberal, anti-humain."[16] God must be
abolished to clear the decks for "la foi nouvelle." Then man can
become the master of creation. It is not without significance that
this man of letters, who went from studying Hebrew and annotating
the Scriptures to glorifying Satan and vilifying God, declared in 1860
(several years after Donoso's death) that Europe was living in an
age of dissolution, and that his "new program" was not yet ready to
be accepted by the masses.[17] If his presuppositions are accepted,
there is a deadly logic to Proudhon's thought. He was very much a
counter-Donoso — and Donoso himself seems to have realized this.
Proudhon's logic did not escape Marx, whose disciples would continue to wage a harsh struggle against Proudhon's followers. Some
years later — in 1871, during the seventy-two-day reign of the Paris
Commune — Proudhon's influence was still greatly in evidence, as
it had been during the exacerbations of 1848.

Most thinkers of the epoch were aware of the close relations
between political and artistic movements, and of the importance of
symbolism in all efforts to replace and in effect destroy traditional
religious myth. Philosophers were lionized by the bourgeoisie, while
journalists — as yet just on the fringe of respectability — tilted
toward revolution. Both groups helped fire the 1848 revolutions.[18]
The boundaries between philosopher and journalist were often nebulous. Even before Marx tried his hand as editor of the *Rheinische
Zeitung,* printers such as Wetling and Becker had, in the early 1840s,
begun socialist publications in Switzerland. Journalism became one
of the most important professional activities for revolutionaries.
They considered an editor to be a sort of lay cleric, his mission the
advancement of the revolution. The union of journalism with the
telegraph produced new and far-reaching possibilities which fascinated many thinkers, including both Marx and Donoso.

16. Löwith, pp. 63-65.
17. Löwith, p. 232.
18. Billington, pp. 306-23.

6

The proliferation of media, the rise of parliamentarianism, the seemingly endless diffusion of placards, flyleaves, posters, and manifestos made their mark on society. From the eye, this infatuation with political discussion moved on to the ear and evolved into debate; discussion became authoritative, rationalism its ground and justification. But as Donoso observed, a society based on discussion is open to argument and closed to everything else. It rejects exception in every form. In Schmitt's words, the society surrounding Donoso "banished the miracle from the world"[19] in its quest to reach the final realization of the spirit: everlasting discussion, endless chatter.

In a society of this type, the bourgeoisie is committed to freedom of speech and freedom of the press to the point where, in effect, this commitment becomes their religion. Nevertheless, this ideal of the peaceful agreement — one that consists simply of convenient, nonviolent arrangements with profits for all — has major disadvantages, as does the displacement of political activity to the level of talk: in the press, in the parliament, in the streets. In Donoso's opinion, this transformation renders society nothing more than a gigantic club where truth arises automatically from discussion or from its surrogate, the vote. The parliamentary state is in reality a glittering facade cloaking vicious internecine struggles of factions and minorities.

The bourgeoisie was best represented by the heirs of Philippe Egalité, who was guillotined on November 6, 1793, despite his serpentine efforts to adapt to the spirit of the times. His son, King Louis Philippe, who had saved his life at that time by defecting along with General Dumouriez, attempted to prop up his regime by distributing government posts to members of the press — and, oddly enough, by glorifying Napoleon. His actions reproduced on a larger scale what his father had attempted. The result was unfortunate, albeit unbloody. It must be admitted, in any case, that Louis Philippe added a certain sensual refinement and preciosity to post-revolutionary France. But as one would expect, when the monarch fled, the intellectuals and journalists remained.

19. Schmitt, *Interpretación,* pp. 36, 53.

7

The preceding observations are intended to provide a sketch of the flora and fauna of the times, a backdrop against which to view the life and thought of Donoso Cortés. Many of these theories reached Donoso in the attenuated, if not distorted, form which most things take when they cross the Pyrenees. However, he would later encounter the genuine articles during his self- imposed Parisian exile and the later diplomatic career which would take him to Berlin and Paris.

It should be noted that Donoso, even at the height of his enthusiasm for liberal French thought, was never an ideological expatriot. His turn away from liberalism was a progressive appropriation and an elevation to consciousness of his national heritage. This Spaniard "de carne y hueso" certainly encountered his roots; the problem was that he attempted to express this encounter in an alien philosophical idiom.

Donoso was in frank opposition to the world generated by the 1789 revolution. He attacked deism, atheism, anti-Christian ideologies, any reduction of Christianity to a mere step toward a higher reality. His belief in original sin and its depredations stood out in stark contrast to the thesis of the naturally good man. In his hard-nosed moral realism, he scoffed at the very notion of the "beautiful soul." As the historian he aspired to be, Donoso gave short shrift to such concepts as the state of nature, the coming golden age, or the perfect society. A fleeting glance at the slaughter-bench of history would dispel such illusions. His elegance, aesthetic sensitivity, and love of traditional pageantry kept him from being attracted by the contrived theatricality of revolution and its often blasphemous symbolism. He came to view the bourgeoisie as a bridge between monarchy and socialism, and discussion as the most effective instrument for the corruption of society. Feminism he abhorred, as he believed the patriarchal family to be the necessary support of society and civilization. Finally, Donoso rejected pacifism, both because of his positive assessment of war and because of his view that pacifism was a chimera which ignored the exigencies of human nature.

Donoso was not an academic philosopher; strictly speaking, he was not even a scholar. Like Augustine, he was interested in all the problems that most professionals have little, if any, desire to investigate. Like Augustine and Nietzsche, his life was inextricably bound to his thought. He was primarily an agonistic man — a fighter, not a detached observer taking notes at a distance — someone in his element in speeches and letters. Nevertheless, his thought is not a mere pastiche of occasional pieces. It has a definite structure and principle of organization. Viewed in retrospect, it can be interpreted as a series of steps moving toward a final goal. Because of this, it is necessary to consider Donoso's thought within the context of the movement of his life, while taking into account the vicissitudes of history and the often arbitrary turns of fortune.

CHAPTER TWO

Youth — Student — Activist

Juan Donoso Cortés was born on May 6, 1809, near Don Benito (at the Valle de la Serena, in the rugged province of Extramadura), when his family was fleeing from the French. The small town of Don Benito, where he grew up, is not far from Medellín, the birthplace of Hernán Cortés, the famous conqueror of Mexico. Not surprisingly, a family tradition traced the Donoso lineage back to an aunt of the conquistador. His parents were comfortable, but scarcely illustrious. His father, Don Martín Cortés, rose from a "vecino labrador y grangero" to become a lawyer and landowner with several commercial interests. María Elena Fernández Cañedo, his mother, was known as "la niña del millón";[1] she was born of wealthy parents, notable within provincial society.

Don Martín was religious in the traditional manner of Spanish men, in which character formation is placed above piety. He was influenced by the ideas of the French Enlightenment, and was a close friend of the liberal leader D. Manuel Quintana, who was at one time confined in rural exile at Cabeza de Buey, just east of Don

---

1. Edmund Schramm, *Donoso Cortés, su Vida y su Pensamiento,* trans. Ramó de la Serna (Madrid: Espasa-Calpe, 1936), pp. 14-15.

Benito. Don Martín hired a tutor from Madrid, Antonio Beltrán, who taught the Donoso children some Latin, French, and other subjects which might be required for entrance to the university. Don Martín kept a watchful, perhaps overly scrupulous, eye on his seven children, of whom Juan was the eldest. (Many years later, when Juan had become ambassador to Paris, we find him complaining to his brother Paco about Don Martín's interference in his affairs.[2]) In any case, Don Martín was a man of advanced views. He allowed Juan to read prohibited French books, belonged to the liberal Sociedad Económica of the Cáceres province, and intervened marginally in politics.[3]

While Juan was often at odds with his father, he was very close to his mother. Family tradition pictures her as able and energetic, a skillful mediator in family disputes. Yet little is known about this good woman. (Much the same can be said of the woman Juan would later marry.) That family conflicts may have led to strained relations is suggested by the fact that Juan departed at such an early age (he was only eleven) to study at Salamanca.

In the autumn of 1820, the university at Salamanca was a center of French Enlightenment. It was at that time under the influence of the philosophies of Destutt-Tracy and Bentham; the novel attractions of constitutionalism, materialism, and radicalism were enthusiastically discussed. Many prominent men of a liberal-progressive tilt, including Manuel José Quintana, had studied in this venerable institution.

After a year or so, Donoso left Salamanca to attend the Colegio de San Pedro de Cáceres, which had (provisionally) acquired the status of a provincial university. At about this time, he met Quintana, who became his unofficial mentor. Don Manuel is described by Schramm as the very personification of liberalism. Greatly influenced by the *Encyclopaedia,* which he had the reputation of having

2. Schramm, p. 13.
3. Schramm, p. 14; John T. Graham, *Donoso Cortés: Utopian Romanticist and Political Realist* (Columbia: University of Missouri Press, 1974), pp. 20-24.

memorized, he was a fighter for all the "good things" of the day: freedom, progress, culture, and tolerance.[4]

On January 19, 1823, Donoso began his studies at the School of Law of the University of Seville. This legendary city was his place of residence, perhaps of romantic initiation, and the point of departure for his fantasies for over four years. He left during the summer of 1828, presumably having graduated.

The Seville residence marks an aesthetic parenthesis in Donoso's life. He tried his hand at poetry and drama, keeping some of his writings in a notebook he called *Poesías de varios amigos*. Following the lead of Quintana and such other prominent liberals as Martínez de la Rosa, he wrote a tragedy about Padilla, the head of the Castilian *comuneros* of the sixteenth century, considered in the nineteenth century to have been a precursor of its movements for liberty. At Seville, Donoso made enduring friendships with Pacheco, Bravo Murillo, and Gallardo, and joined a group called "Sons of Apollo."[5] We find in his early works, many written under the pseudonym of "Delio," a heavy baroque style joined to a youthful naïveté that all too often passes into silliness. Politically, these initial works are openly reflective of their milieu. They are liberal and francophile, favoring the trendy enterprises of the day.

When Gallardo and Pacheco proposed the establishment of a literary and philosophical academy (perhaps a high-tone version of a "tertulia"), Donoso replied, with youthful arrogance, that he had read both the "sensualists" (Locke, Condillac, and Destutt-Tracy) and the "traditionalists" (Bonald) and had already surpassed them both.[6] Graham is right in stating that Donoso suffered from an "inflated intellectualism,"[7] though a strong trace of the whimsical arbitrariness of the Spanish señorito can also be noted. Donoso's pontificating was not to the liking of Pacheco, who found his re-

4. Schramm, p. 27.

5. Graham, p. 26.

6. *Obras Completas de Don Juan Donoso Cortés,* ed. Carlos Valverde (Madrid: BAC, 1970), vol. 1, pp. 173-75.

7. Graham, p. 26.

marks ill-humored, rude, and unduly aggressive[8] — accusations that would be repeated, often with reason, over the course of his career.

After a brief and possibly frustrating visit to Madrid, where he arrived armed with a letter of introduction from Quintana, Donoso returned home and worked in his father's law office for about two years. He began to read voluminously, albeit capriciously, judging from a notebook he kept at the time. This notebook includes observations on Rousseau, Machiavelli, Voltaire, Madame de Staël, Montaigne, Montesquieu, Chateaubriand, Byron, and others, and ends with an agenda of further readings. Most surprising is the paucity of Spanish authors: only *La Celestina* and some of Calderón's dramas are included.[9] When Cáceres was again upgraded to the status of a university, the Chair of Aesthetics and Politics was offered to Manuel José Quintana. He declined, but recommended Donoso, who accepted with typical hauteur. He refused to use manuals, and he refused to teach either history or geography, so that he could concentrate on teaching "the most fruitful principles of literature and its most brilliant exponents."[10]

The Colegio de Humanidades de Cáceres must have been quite a modest enterprise: it was inaugurated, in October of 1829, with a lecture by Donoso, who was all of twenty years old. This lecture is a display that Schramm calls "brilliant and pretentious" and Graham calls a "liberal-romantic manifesto."[11] It is, in fact, both. Here Donoso broaches several themes which will later be developed and become points of departure for future speculation. He praises enthusiasm as a reflection of the priority of poetry and feeling over philosophy and reason. Moreover, he postulates a natural inclination in mankind toward the heroic, the just, and the beautiful.[12] Although Donoso savages feudalism as "el árbol monstruoso," he has

8. Schramm, p. 37.
9. Schramm, pp. 44-45.
10. *Obras,* vol. 1.
11. Schramm, pp. 47-49; Graham, p. 28.
12. *Obras,* vol. 1, pp. 183-85 and 193.

kind words for the papacy and praises the crusades for having introduced enthusiasm into Europe, thus making the virtues burgeon. More interestingly, Donoso asserts that the Middle Ages brought about a withdrawal into the self, the "moral self." This allowed the Christian to engage in moral combat and moved the center of gravity from acts to character.[13] This change constituted a moral revolution which fixed the boundaries between ancient and modern civilization.

Donoso also credits Christianity with providing the stimulus necessary for the civilizing of the "melancholy and ferocious northern barbarians."[14] Moreover, he adumbrates his later attacks on rationalism by inveighing against "la filosofía de las sensaciones" (empiricism). He traces a line of descent from Bacon through Locke and Condillac to Helvétius, where "empiricism" becomes "disfigured" and begins to "rave." According to Donoso, this philosophical school is largely responsible for the climate of dispute flooding Europe and has reversed the turn effected by the Middle Ages. It has expelled man from the fortress of his "moral ego" into the chaos of the external world. Nonetheless, Donoso praises the nineteenth century. It is, he says, marching confidently on the path of Enlightenment, joining the wisdom of the past to the experience of the present.[15]

Despite its many weaknesses, among which intellectual hubris and pedagogical bombast are not the least, this is a remarkable performance. The content, while not original, is interesting — almost exceptional, given the circumstances, though it is nearly buried by its baroque facade. Donoso rambles, gushes unashamedly, and never fails to make an unnecessary dramatic gesture. This address was the dramatic prelude to a rather dismal professorial career. His lectures attracted only two students, and only one of them persevered. The survivor, Gabino Tejado, would become a good friend, and later the editor of Donoso's works. He also translated the works

13. *Obras,* vol. 1, pp. 190-91.
14. *Obras,* vol. 1, p. 193.
15. *Obras,* vol. 1, pp. 198-99, 202-3.

of Manzini and became a noted Catholic apologist, outliving his teacher by nearly forty years.[16]

In 1830, Donoso married Dna. Teresa Carrasco. It was a tragic marriage. She died only five years later, and was preceded in death by their only child, María. The hints and clues which have come down to us say very little except that Teresa was retiring and physically rather unattractive. In later life, Donoso told his friend Louis Veuillot of the great sorrow he had experienced when Teresa died, and he spoke of her (in accents which compare favorably with Patmore's "Angel in the House") as "the purest soul who ever lived on earth." At the time of her death, he spoke of her "celestial image" in a letter to her parents.[17] It might be suggested that the "cordeur et l'humilité" which he ascribed to his wife are scarcely characteristics he would have so fervently admired as a young man. These later remarks were probably colored by distance and possibly by guilt — by a need to stress those virtues which he had come to admire only after a lifetime of political, diplomatic, and religious struggle.

Juan Donoso Cortés was born into a period of change, the tumultuous era in which Spain was caught in the aftermath of the French Revolution. The return to power of King Fernando VII, the one-time "deseado," inaugurated a return to strict monarchy. Spain was now divided into two major camps: the liberals, who sympathized with the revolution, and the absolutists, who were clerical and traditional. While the king oscillated between the two camps, his brother Carlos, the heir apparent, was firmly on the side of the absolutists. The picture changed radically, though, when Fernando married his fourth wife, María Cristina de Borbón. Most of the portraits show her as a somewhat bovine woman with intelligent eyes. However, Vicente Lopez's portrait is favorable to the queen; his canvas reflects, in a modest way, her reputation as a great beauty.[18]

---

16. Schramm, p. 51 n. 2.
17. Schramm, p. 53.
18. Ramón Menéndez Pidal, *Historia de España,* vol. 34: *La Era Isabelina y el Sexenio Democrático* [1834-1874] (Madrid: Espasa-Calpe, 1981), p. 49, fig. 17.

Two children were born to the royal couple: the future Isabel II and the Infanta Luisa Fernanda. On March 19, 1830, prodded by María Cristina and her equally forceful sister, Fernando VII issued a Pragmatic Sanction modifying the law of inheritance. It reversed the French Salic Law, originally established in Spain by Philip V, the first Bourbon king, in 1713. Under pressure from Don Carlos's supporters, Fernando revoked the Pragmatic Sanction when he fell gravely ill; however, as soon as he recovered, he had this decree annulled. The king's last testament (June 1830) made María Cristina guardian of their children and regent-governor of Spain as long as they were still minors. After Fernando's death she retained Cea Bermúdez as head of government, and on October 23, 1833, she granted an amnesty which extended to some prominent liberals.[19]

The way for María Cristina's ascent to power had been prepared by General Llauder's purge of conservative elements, which was concentrated on those affiliated with the pro-Carlist Royal Volunteers. The others were given the coup de grace by the legislation of October 23, which disarmed the Volunteers and established a new militia. The stage was set for the First Carlist War (1833-1840), which was marked by extraordinary ferocity, cruelty, and heroism. By the end of 1833, over seventy towns had declared for Don Carlos. The Carlists were in control of Vizcaya and had penetrated into Guipuzcoa, Alava, and Santander.[20]

As Graham has indicated, the July revolution in France and the dynastic problems in Spain made 1830 a propitious year for Donoso to enter politics. Together with his brothers-in-law, Donoso plunged into "forbidden political activities." They undertook to organize "Cristino" groups to agitate in favor of María Cristina, Isabel, and a constitution.[21] With a sharp eye for political opportunity, Donoso,

19. Menéndez Pidal, pp. 71-72. See also John F. Coverdale, *The Basque Phase of Spain's First Carlist War* (Princeton: Princeton University Press, 1984), pp. 122-23.

20. Coverdale, pp. 127-28.

21. Graham, p. 32.

on October 13, 1832, directed to the king a *memoria* defending the Pragmatic Sanction as an authentic reflection of Spain's ancient law of female succession.[22] It was a fortunate stroke. The king (actually the queen) had the memorandum published in a luxury edition; and after Fernando's death on September 29, 1833, Donoso was given the modest but high-sounding post of "Secretario con Ejercicio de Decretos" in the "Gracia y Justicia de Indias" department of the Secretariat of State.

The hostilities between the Cristinos and the Carlistas in reality consisted of a struggle between the bourgeois revolution and its opponents. At the time, this struggle was viewed (erroneously) by outside observers as a revolt of the lower classes, despite the fact that its most fervent supporters were the clergy and peasantry.[23] Donoso launched harsh attacks on Don Carlos and his followers, although they advocated principles that he would later support. The Carlists stood for legitimacy, fidelity to traditional values, the virtues of the countryside, and "fueros" — local privileges and immunities — which they believed were endangered by the Madrid government's drive toward uniformity and centralization. All this was united to a sacral view of the world, a view which Donoso could easily have endorsed.[24]

When Don Carlos crossed from France into Spain on July 12, 1834 — after having failed to enter from Portugal and having been forced to seek refuge in England — the Madrid mobs reacted by effecting a horrifying massacre of friars (July 17-18) and then attacking other religious houses. Their pretext was the venerable canard about the victims' having poisoned the wells, causing the plague. Donoso protested, at first somewhat mutely, and went on to write a second *memoria,* this time addressed to María Cristina. If later developments can be used as criteria, it was probably favorably received

22. "Memoria sobre la situación actual de la Monarquía," *Obras,* vol. 1, pp. 213-24.

23. Menéndez Pidal, pp. 107-8.

24. Coverdale, pp. 303-5.

by the Queen Regent, though this memorandum — unlike his first one — did not produce immediate results.

More eventful was his pamphlet *Consideraciones sobre la Diplomacia,* published in August 1834. Donoso was one of the few Spanish thinkers of his day who dedicated serious attention to the subject of diplomacy. His first work on the subject, this is no tightly knit, well-reasoned treatise. It begins with one of those vast historical panoramas in which Donoso took so much delight. This panorama comes complete with extensive commentary, some side glances at people and events, and, of course, the requisite bows in the direction of María Cristina. He often seems to be following his pen, and his pen seems to be following his mouth. (In several of his works, the pen becomes even more obviously a mere verbal surrogate.)

That the *Consideraciones* is written under the influence of French thought — Guizot, Cousin, Constant, Destutt-Tracy, perhaps even Saint-Simon — is evidenced by Donoso's enthusiastic acceptance of the "principle of intelligence," his belief in human perfectibility and in the superiority of ideas over force, and his appeal to the Tribunal of Reason. Nevertheless, he does castigate severely the mob responsible for the anticlerical depredations of July, as well as the government which failed to intervene with any real energy. Sparks of what is to come are noticeable in, for example, his encomium of religion as the basis of society, and of suffering as the crucible of human perfection.

López-Cordon correctly observes that the major theme of the pamphlet is the idea of intelligence — to be exact, the "principle of intelligence."[25] Conquest, Donoso urges, takes place not because of material interests, but because of ideas that reflect principles. What makes all the difference is ideas, not material force. When an idea loses its vitality, even the greatest of men (he names Alexander, Mohammed, and Napoleon) fade into obscurity. Intelligence is the legitimate ruler of society. Each period of history is defined by an

25. María Victoria López-Cordon Cortezo, "La Política Exterior," in *Historia de España,* vol. 34, pp. 838-43.

idea. But although intelligence, which can at times be equated with justice, automatically rules in the moral world, it must be buttressed by force to reign in society. When intelligence reigns, society becomes its instrument in the advance toward human perfectibility: a goal which cannot be frustrated.[26]

This quasi-Hegelianism has a definite practical tilt. Though unadulterated force leads to tyranny, ideas must be converted into facts *(hechos)* so that they can struggle with, and finally replace, the previous facts which impeded their advance. Force is legitimatized as the necessary means for the idea to prevail. Diplomacy is nothing less than the expression of intelligence and progress in the moral order. It replaces force as the means to the desired end and testifies to the presence of a higher degree of civilization.[27]

Donoso will later denounce the principle of intelligence as the concoction of a debased and corrupting bourgeoisie. But at this point, he is still lauding the bourgeoisie as "queen of the universe."[28] Moving to praxis, Donoso praises the recent Quadruple Alliance formed to combat the claims of Don Carlos and Dom Miguel, the Portuguese pretender. This, he says, is the "first diplomatic protest worthy of civilization."[29] Although Austria, Prussia, and Russia were also inclined toward Don Carlos, only Naples and Turin had recognized his claims. To forestall a burgeoning of Carlist support, France, Britain, Spain, and Portugal entered into this alliance — a definite triumph for the Madrid government. The practical results, however, were negligible, aside from the formation of French and British "legions" which failed to become effective fighting units.

Here we first encounter Donoso of the pithy comment, the outrageous description, the overembroidered phrase, the lucid insight. England conquers, he says, not by exerting military might, but by dividing its enemies. Don Carlos is "a disloyal prince burdened with

26. *Obras,* vol. 1, pp. 232, 258, 270, and 274.
27. *Obras,* vol. 1, pp. 232, 285.
28. *Obras,* vol. 1, p. 280.
29. *Obras,* vol. 1, pp. 272-73.

ignominy and overwhelmed by the weight of the maledictions of his fatherland." While righteously and mistakenly stating that despotism has become impossible in Europe, and while castigating Dom Miguel of Portugal as "a monster embracing a skeleton in the depths of a tomb," he goes on making his usual compliments to the august Queen María Cristina.[30] Exaggeration was, no doubt, appropriate to his age, country, and profession. Yet one cannot but surmise that Donoso took it to new extremes.

This may have reflected a certain split in his personality which was noted by friends, enemies, and even himself. López-Cordon sees evidence of this split in his work: she notes, for instance, a gap between the "pragmatic negotiator" and the "tormented futuristic theoretician."[31] But perhaps we should not take the young Donoso too seriously. What is really surprising is that Donoso's liberal, francophile leanings did not take him further down the garden path toward revolution. Even at this early date, small fissures can be detected in his liberalism which will lead eventually to the destruction of the entire edifice.

The treatise was extravagantly praised and harshly criticized. One of Donoso's contemporaries accused him of both plagiarism and francophilia.[32] Donoso counterattacked in a lengthy missive, dated September 30, 1834. In this missive, he excuses himself because of his youth and takes the critic to task for failing to realize that France is the doyen of European civilization; to prove his point, he then embarks on a lengthy analysis of the Middle Ages and the Italian wars. Regarding the plagiarism charge, he counters by declaring that if everyone who fails to discover a "new idea" is a plagiarist, then he is ready to plead guilty. But this would as well apply to his critic's "master," Jeremy Bentham, who discovered absolutely nothing. Donoso then overstates his case by citing Plato (on recollection) out of context and by proclaiming himself "the voice of the nineteenth century."[33]

30. *Obras,* vol. 1, pp. 245, 255, 258, 268, and 279.
31. López-Cordon, pp. 838-43.
32. *Obras,* vol. 1, p. 282 n. 1.
33. *Obras,* vol. 1, pp. 287-88.

Toward the end of this apologia, Donoso hits upon the interesting theme of language and its many problems — a theme that will be found, at least implicitly, in many of his later writings. He defends his emulation of the French by arguing that the Castilian tongue has never been domesticated by a philosopher (a complaint later echoed by philosophers of the stature of Ortega and Zubiri). Castilian simply lacks a literary or philosophical style appropriate to the nineteenth century. Although purists attempt to concoct a style by emulating that of the "Golden Age," this style cannot be used to express ideas relevant to the present. A mummy cannot be resuscitated. Donoso urges that there are only two viable options: create a new style, or adopt a living philosophical language. He chose the latter.[34] A similar difficulty had been mentioned in the prologue to his most ambitious poetic work, "El Cerco de Zamora"; there he discussed the problems encountered by moderns in their attempt to comprehend the language of the ancient world.[35]

The political scene remained turbulent. The Carlist War gained momentum. By the spring of 1835, the Carlist general Zumalacárregui had won several impressive victories and had succeeded in baffling the Cristino generals sent against him. By order of Don Carlos, but against his better judgment, he undertook the siege of Bilbao. Zumalacárregui was wounded; on June 24, 1835, he died of complications.[36]

On the home front, the government of Mendizábal formulated drastic anticlerical legislation which greatly affected both the economic and social orders, creating an aggressive middle class. In March 1836, when the new Cortes took their seats, the moderate party to which Donoso was affiliated made its first appearance. A few months later, on August 13, the revolt of La Granja took place. Troops invaded the palace and forced the Queen Regent to reestablish the liberal constitution of Cádiz. Donoso, at the time still *persona*

34. *Obras,* vol. 1, p. 289.
35. Schramm, pp. 72-73.
36. Coverdale, pp. 220-21.

grata to the liberals, was promoted by Mendizábal to the post of Cabinet Secretary ("Secretario del Gabinete y de la Presidencia del Consejo"), and was elected deputy for Badajoz in the Cortes.[37]

37. Schramm, pp. 78-80.

CHAPTER THREE

Doctrinaire Liberal

After 1836 Spanish liberals were divided into two factions: the progressives, who tilted toward the left and revolution, and the moderates, who were bourgeois and monarchical. Suárez indicates that the progressives were prone to violence and intellectually inferior to the moderates, the party of the middle class and the aristocracy.[1] The moderates were accused of pessimism and a lack of confidence in human nature — characteristics later made notorious by Donoso. Until the 1860s, however, the moderates were the most important political party in Spain.[2] Both parties had intellectual centers in Madrid. The Ateneo played a key role in the plans of the moderates; the Liceo, in those of the progressives. The lectures and courses given in each of these centers were part of a wider plan to elaborate a political philosophy; but the efforts of both parties were only partially successful. Donoso, Galiano, Pidal, and other moderates used the Ateneo to publicize their attempts to modify liberal ideology by resolving the tension between order and freedom in favor of order.[3]

1. Federico Suárez Verdeguer, *Introducción a Donoso Cortés* (Madrid: Rialp, 1964), pp. 23-24, 44-46.
2. Ramón Menéndez Pidal, *Historia de España,* vol. 34: *La Era Isabeline y el Sexenio Democrático [1834-1874]* (Madrid: Espasa-Calpe, 1981), p. 381.
3. Menéndez Pidal, vol. 34, pp. 401-2.

Ensconced in the political establishment, on good terms with the *Reina Gobernadora* and the circle which surrounded her, Donoso was in a superb position to advance his interests. The Ateneo invited him to give a series of lectures on constitutional law in place of the recently exiled Alcalá Galiano, a liberal anti-absolutist who had fallen into disfavor after the Granja mutiny. Donoso accepted. He gave a series of evening lectures centered on the theme of sovereignty — lectures which mark the high point of his liberalism and at the same time show evidence of his later conservative turn. The lectures were not finished; they were discontinued by the Calatrava government.

These lectures have been treated rather cavalierly by critics ever since they were delivered (1836-1837). At the time, Gallardo criticized Donoso as a "guizotín" and a plagiarist of Royer-Collard; he even accused Donoso of aping the Frenchman's pseudo-apocalyptic style.[4] The gibe was malicious, but not outrageous. In the introduction to his English translation of these lectures, Professor Vincent McNamara classifies the Donoso of that time as a doctrinal liberal in the line of Royer-Collard, Guizot, de Broglie, and Remusat — a group characterized by theoretical eclecticism and a middle-of-the-road position in social and political issues under the standard of the principle of intelligence.[5] Graham refers to these lectures as "the *magnum opus* of Donoso's liberal years"[6] — a fairly safe evaluation, to be sure.

Donoso begins and ends these lectures with a romantic eulogy of youth: it is the young people who are the prophets, priests, and martyrs of revolution. From them come the new ideas; it is they who

---

4. Edmund Schramm, *Donoso Cortés, su Vida y su Pensamiento,* trans. Ramón de la Serna (Madrid: Espasa-Calpe, 1936), pp. 95-96.

5. Juan Donoso Cortés, *A Defense of Representative Government,* trans. with introduction and notes by Vincent McNamara (North York: Captus, 1991), pp. v-vi, xix. See *Obras Completus de Don Juan Donoso Cortés,* ed. Carlos Valverde (Madrid: BAC, 1970), vol. 1, pp. 327, 445.

6. John T. Graham, *Donoso Cortés: Utopian Romanticist and Political Realist* (Columbia: University of Missouri Press, 1974), pp. 42-44.

will forge the world of the future. Committed to purging the earth of monsters, they march fearlessly between inquisitor and executioner, pyre and guillotine.[7] There is more here than naive bombast. Donoso rejects the "state of nature," insisting that society is a "primitive fact" derived from the principle of intelligence. But intelligence is opposed to freedom. Intelligence is social, freedom antisocial. The first attracts; the second repels. This opposition must be resolved.

There is a way to resolve this opposition, a way to protect both society and freedom against disruption. The solution is provided by government, which should strive to preserve both society and freedom. But government is subordinated to the sovereign. So the question to be asked is, "Who is sovereign?" There are three possible solutions: society absorbs the individual, the individual absorbs society, or the individual and society coexist. Donoso sees these three solutions as being articulated, respectively, by the divine right of kings, popular sovereignty, and the principle of intelligence. However, he says, divine right and popular sovereignty, though radically opposed, are both types of despotism. It follows that the principle of intelligence, reflected in representative government, is the only viable option. But in order to be successful, government must be capable of surmounting many problems, the most serious one being that of preserving society without unduly repressing the individuals which compose it.[8]

Donoso distinguishes between two sovereignties: that of fact and that of right. Sovereignty of fact is the constituted authority; sovereignty of right is the ground and raison d'être of that authority. Donoso constructs an apologia for representative government by tracing the development of the principle of intelligence in history. He outlines the process of its secularization; it reached completion, he says, when Luther emancipated intelligence from theology. But unfortunately, this emancipation created a seedbed for revolution, a

7. Donoso Cortés, *Defense,* lecture 7, p. 76, and lecture 1, p. 5; *Obras,* vol. 1, pp. 403-31.

8. *Defense,* lecture 1, pp. 8-9; *Obras,* vol. 1, p. 334.

situation exploited by Rousseau. In Donoso's opinion, Rousseau was not a philosopher but a prophet, "the terrifying personification of the masses."[9] The principle of popular sovereignty, says Donoso, triumphed in the French Revolution and generated a new epoch — one which has, in effect, destroyed the work of twelve centuries.

To rule, insists Donoso, is a function of reason. It follows, therefore, that society should be ruled by the most intelligent, and that because of, and in accord with, the variation among intelligences, it should be hierarchically structured. Democracy is based, not on intelligence, but on the will: democracy is by definition egalitarian, and all wills are equal. Karl Popper agrees with Donoso's criticism of Plato for having formulated the prototypical theory of despotism.[10] In Donoso's rather fanciful depiction, Plato sacrificed Greek to Oriental genius, proclaimed the unity and trinity of God, held other bizarre views, and was therefore like an "Egyptian statue placed in the Parthenon."[11]

Having thus disposed of Plato, Donoso vaults over two millennia to Bonald, a French traditionalist who echoed Plato, however remotely, in his formulation of a more structured theory of despotism based on Christian belief. Donoso has little sympathy for this vast authoritarian structure which boasts, among other things, a universal system of education administered by the Jesuits.[12] Admittedly, such a system does preserve order; but it is the order of the tomb. Everything is lost except hope.

Donoso's overarching view of history postulates a three-stage advance: (1) theocracy, the primitive form of despotism; (2) democracy, absolute independence; and (3) representative government, the system that advances the sovereignty of intelligence and the perfectibility of man. Primitive theocracy was later resuscitated on both a higher level, by the Roman pontiffs, and on a lower

9. *Defense,* lecture 2, pp. 12-13; *Obras,* vol. 1, pp. 344-45.
10. Karl Popper, *The Open Society and Its Enemies* (London: Routledge, 1945).
11. *Defense,* lecture 3, pp. 25-27; lecture 9, pp. 90-91; *Obras,* vol. 1, pp. 352-53, 417-19.
12. *Defense,* lecture 3, pp. 30-31; *Obras,* vol. 1, p. 357.

level, by the divine right of kings. The latter, urges Donoso, is a blasphemy which was justly punished by revolution.[13]

It is revealing that at this early, liberal stage of his life, Donoso (at times, it seems, irreflectively) views political and social problems from a theological perspective. Not only is his cast of mind religious, but theology becomes the ultimate court of appeal for the weightiest matters. In these lectures, for example, both popular sovereignty and divine right are attacked as immoral, subversive, and absurd because they despoil God of omnipotence. Moreover, both require passive obedience from their subjects, an obedience which is indistinguishable from slavery. Both are "dogmas of social omnipotence," an omnipotence identified with sovereignty of right, so they are really just two heads of a single monster. Absolute monarchy is despotism by one man; democracy is despotism by an entire people.[14]

The desideratum is to achieve a balance between intelligence, which makes government possible, and freedom, which makes the individual possible. To arrive at this balance, society must respect omnipotence as belonging to no one but God, who is "the personification of all truths."[15] The earthly sovereign will then be viewed as limited, and his subjects as enjoying rights. Both sovereign and subjects will see themselves as they are: as fragile beings before God. Limited reason should be reflected by limited authority. But though reason is limited in all human beings, it is so in different degrees. Donoso can then conclude that "the most intelligent has the right to command, and the less intelligent the obligation to obey."[16] Fatuous and naive as it sounds today, this variation on Royer-Collard could well have served as the credo of most middle-of-the-road young intellectuals of the day. It was a potent theory adhered to by quite reputable thinkers, including the French eclectics. Donoso's

13. *Defense,* lecture 3, pp. 35, 39, and 41-42; lecture 5, pp. 45-46; *Obras,* vol. 1, pp. 368-69.

14. *Defense,* lecture 5, pp. 46-47; *Obras,* vol. 1, pp. 373-74.

15. *Defense,* lecture 6, p. 60; *Obras,* vol. 1, p. 387.

16. *Defense,* lecture 6, p. 61; lecture 7, pp. 65-66; *Obras,* vol. 1, pp. 389, 391-92.

variation, its flaws admitted, is scarcely the weakest, though his attempt at providing it with a theoretical scaffolding falls short of the mark.

The principle of intelligence follows the transformations of society, which passes by degrees from a spontaneous to a reflective state. The Roman Empire was able to conquer other peoples because it surpassed them in intelligence. Later, Christianity deposited the "germ" of intelligence in the barbarian tribes by means of the sword of Charlemagne. It then moved from the medieval schools to the universities, on to the poets, and, in the fifteenth century, into the palaces. Intelligence was constantly on the move, and by the eighteenth century it had begun to move into homes, workshops, and public places. Finally, in Donoso's own century, intelligence is "conquering the middle class, which in its name is seeking the scepter of the world."[17]

A regressive movement begins with the introduction of deism and materialism into Europe — a movement of which the French Revolution was the bloody commentary.[18] But this was not, says Donoso, an unmitigated disaster. It was the providential occasion for the emergence of eclecticism, which in the political realm is now reflected by the doctrinaire school engaged in the arduous task of reorganizing society. Donoso cites Royer-Collard, Guizot, and de Broglie, affirming that even revolution is legitimate if grounded on the authority of intelligence. In any case, the eclectic school presents a positive option, avoiding as it does the extremes of divine right and popular sovereignty.[19] However, a different note is sounded in the last lecture, which ends with a surprising encomium of the strong man who defends truth even among the ruins[20] — scarcely a fitting epilogue to the position he is defending.

These lectures are diffuse, rambling, prone to stopping at unnec-

17. *Defense,* lecture 7, pp. 71-72; lecture 8, pp. 82-83, 87-88; *Obras,* vol. 1, pp. 398-99, 416.

18. *Defense,* lecture 9, pp. 95-96; *Obras,* vol. 1, pp. 423-24.

19. *Defense,* lecture 9, pp. 96-99; *Obras,* vol. 1, pp. 424-26.

20. *Defense,* lecture 10, p. 116; *Obras,* vol. 1, p. 445.

essary ports of call, often repetitious, intermittently inane, usually pompous. Yet they are interspersed with acute observations and surprising insights, and they are shot through with a serious attempt to impose structure on a disparate collection of material and a theme lacking consistency. And even some of the most unfortunate of Donoso's observations are not lacking in humor. There is, for example, his pre-Freudian description of atheistic philosophers as "a phalanx of eunuchs . . . [who] . . . reject the mace of Hercules,"[21] and his superbly pedantic depiction of humanity as "the Ulysses of Homer borne by the hand of Minerva across the stormy seas."[22] His praise of Charlemagne is extravagant; his comparison between Moses and Odin, merely incongruous, as is his division of intelligence according to the three ages of man.[23]

These flaws notwithstanding, his distinction between sovereignty of fact and sovereignty of right, though not original, is well employed, and the contrast between the "political skeptic" and the "political puritan" is nicely drawn. His defense of dictatorship is unexpected, an adumbration of his later thought. Dictatorship is a terrible exception appropriate only to periods of cataclysm. The dictator is a strong man who "appears as a divinity. . . . At his appearance . . . the tempests are pacified."[24] The dictator transcends written law and philosophical theory: he is a living protest against both law and philosophy. He is not, however, an exception to the rule of intelligence, but rather its confirmation. As soon as society returns to normality, authority departs from this one intelligent individual and reverts to the most intelligent group.[25] Dictatorship is sometimes necessary as an antidote to social revolution, since only dictatorship can channel the flood of vicious custom, give ideas a new direction, establish the reign of law, and uproot whatever cancer may be devouring society.[26]

21. *Defense,* lecture 6, p. 55; *Obras,* vol. 1, p. 382.
22. *Defense,* lecture 5, p. 51; *Obras,* vol. 1, p. 379.
23. *Defense,* lecture 8, p. 84; *Obras,* vol. 1, pp. 412-13.
24. *Defense,* lecture 6, pp. 62-63; *Obras,* vol. 1, p. 390.
25. *Defense,* lecture 6, p. 63 n. 2; *Obras,* vol. 1, p. 391 n. (a).
26. *Defense,* lecture 10, pp. 112-13; *Obras,* vol. 1, pp. 441-42.

There are other signs that Donoso's liberalism is beginning to wear thin. For example, though he praises the French Revolution several times as a humanitarian event which accelerated the development of intelligence, he rails against the "sophists" who have made France barbarian, transferring responsibility for the nation's destiny from an "intelligent aristocracy" to the "popular masses."[27] Moreover, he treats the reactionary "Catholic School" — the French traditionalists — with exquisite tact, almost with reverence, noting the many eminent writers found in their ranks. He finds their belief that reason dissolves while faith unites (the polar opposite of his own view) "magnificent and majestic, however scorned by the times and the revolutions."[28] Even in the Catholic School, the principle of intelligence is surreptitiously present, notwithstanding the adamant opposition traditionalists seemingly have to both freedom and intelligence.[29]

In retrospect, these antiliberal episodes have obvious significance. To Donoso's contemporaries, however, they were nothing but insignificant blotches on an otherwise liberal canvas. At the time of these lectures, the progressives were taking over the government, putting José María Calatrava in charge; a constitution was drawn up that favored the moderate position; and the authority of General Espartero was increasing. During the period 1836-1840, Donoso's life was marked by intense journalistic activity and by his parliamentary debut. He was contributing to several journals, some on a regular basis. These include *El Porvenir, El Piloto, El Correo Nacional,* and *La Revista de Madrid.*[30] As Donoso's relation to María Cristina flourished, so did his political and intellectual prominence, which would only increase when he followed María Cristina into exile at Paris.

27. *Defense,* lecture 4, p. 41; lecture 6, p. 55; lecture 7, p. 75; *Obras,* vol. 1, pp. 368, 381, and 403.
28. *Defense,* lecture 9, p. 102; *Obras,* vol. 1, pp. 430-32.
29. *Defense,* lecture 9, p. 102; *Obras,* vol. 1, pp. 430-32.
30. Schramm, pp. 99-100.

During these journalistic years, Donoso's retreat from liberalism continues, though at a slow pace. His style becomes sharper, his arguments tighter. His humor moves to the sardonic. His vanity burgeons, to the point that he almost deserves the nickname given him by the satiric *El Guirigay:* "Quiquiriqui" (cock-a-doodle-doo).[31] In these journalistic pieces we encounter flashes which anticipate his later thought: his attacks on reason, revolution, and demagoguery; his defense of Christianity, the crusades, and the *Reconquista.* A new theme makes its appearance: his opposition to the atheistic notion of freedom. This is a pernicious concept, he says, inasmuch as it immures God in the individual conscience and fails to proclaim God publicly by means of cult and law. The French Revolution has fallen another notch in his estimation. Donoso now claims that the revolution was caused by the ascent of the "materialist principle" and the descent of the "religious principle." It was a "bloody commentary" on the emancipation of human reason, an emancipation which he fears is rapidly moving mankind toward self-adoration. According to Fr. Suárez, Donoso in this period is moving away from rationalism, making an increasingly sober assessment of the principle of intelligence, and holding a more negative view of the French Revolution. On the home front, he is beginning to develop an unfavorable opinion of the parliament (Cortes) as an isolated entity, as something dissociated from monarch, church, and people.[32]

Donoso took a seat in the Cortes as deputy from Cádiz. His friends Pacheco and Bravo Murillo joined him there. His first parliamentary intervention took place on March 14, 1838, when he defended the use of a dictator under extraordinary circumstances. When he gave his first discourse seventeen days later, it was a fiasco. He took the topic under consideration — the allocation of moneys for the Carlist war — and attempted to convert it into a prize piece of oratory. Much to the amusement and annoyance of the deputies,

31. Schramm, p. 99 n. 3.
32. Suárez, p. 39.

he pompously cited Mirabeau: "The whole chamber joined to drown out his voice in laughter and clapping."[33]

The major effort Donoso was making — an attempt to have the monarchy based on "legitimate minorities" (the bourgeoisie) — was proving to be futile. His move away from rationalism, on the one hand, and the debacle of several succeeding governments, on the other, persuaded him of its intrinsic weakness. He changed course and attempted to restore to the throne its full measure of authority, which it had not had since 1832. From about 1839 on, we see Donoso beginning to take an increasingly active part in the political life of Spain. In the words of Fr. Suárez, "Donoso becomes a courtesan, a palace creature, and during several years will be a gray eminence who moves . . . the strings of Spanish politics."[34]

The first Carlist War was fought with the extreme ferocity that is typical of fraternal conflict. In spite of rare victories, such as that of Oriamendi, and individual heroics, such as the spectacular feats of General Cabrera, Carlist fortunes waned. It was simply impossible to replace Zumalacárregui. In a final effort, Don Carlos personally led the "royal expedition" into Cristino heartland, reaching the outskirts of Madrid in the middle of September 1837. But no attack was made; the Carlist army simply withdrew. The reason for this incredible decision is still a matter of speculation. Carlist lack of artillery and the failure of a palace intrigue are two of the strongest hypotheses advanced. All that is certain, however, is that the expedition turned north, was defeated in an encounter with Espartero, and arrived at Navarre in late October.[35]

Carlist fortunes continued to decline. (General Cabrera's capture of Morella in 1838 was a notable exception.) Finally, on August 29, 1839, an armistice, still the subject of heated debate among historians, was signed by General Espartero and (Carlist) General Maroto,

33. Graham, p. 48.
34. Suárez, p. 85.
35. John F. Coverdale, *The Basque Phase of Spain's First Carlist War* (Princeton: Princeton University Press, 1984), pp. 290-91; Menéndez Pidal, pp. 93-94.

which, in effect, ended the war. Don Carlos and twenty thousand supporters entered France in September, and General Cabrera followed in July 1840. The war was too cruel, the stakes too high, and the contenders too radically opposed for any kind of peace to last for long. In 1846 an outburst occurred which blazed into a small war in 1848-1849. This struggle, which was almost totally confined to Catalonia, has gone down in the history books as the *guerra dels matiners*.[36]

It was during this four-year period — from the time of the Ateneo lectures to his self-imposed exile in Paris — that Donoso engaged in his first public controversy. Pelegrino Rossi had published an article in Guizot's *La Revue Française* stating that France had a vested interest in the fragmentation of Spanish unity. Donoso took him to task, reminding him that history had definitively fixed European frontiers and that the traditional policy of France favored close relations with Spain. The goal of dismembering Spain had certainly never been adopted by the French Cabinet as a definitive policy.[37] And in any case, this was the nineteenth century, when nations were communicating by means of ideas, not violence.[38] Should there exist any danger to France, it certainly would not come from Spain — the two countries were bonded by the Quadruple Alliance. Whatever danger there might be to France would come from its northern neighbors. Nations devoid of monarchical or aristocratic inclinations were ultimately going to fall into the democratic camp. Contrary to Dr. Rossi's opinion that they would constitute protective battlements for France, these nations were uncertain and hostile elements, pitfalls on the road to a positive future.

The Rossi polemic marks Donoso's initial disenchantment with the "eclectics." Yes, they have indeed proved to be the party of common sense, the mean between the two extremes of French politics. They have succeeded in imposing their ideology through the one medium not subject to oscillation: education.[39] They have

---

36. Menéndez Pidal, p. 135.
37. Donoso Cortés, "Polémica con Rossi," *Obras,* vol. 1, pp. 492-510.
38. "Polémica," p. 508.
39. "Polémica," p. 495.

transformed parliament into theatre, and the academic chair into a throne. But they have been unable to deal with the July revolution and the questions it generated. The eclectics cannot put together a philosophical, political, and social agenda — a dogma.[40] They have been neutered by academicism; they have lost their instinct. And having lost all ability to love and to hate, they have come to regard the throne and the masses as merely two litigants facing a court, of which they themselves are the judges.[41]

Donoso was moving toward a position comparable to what Viereck once called "temperamental conservatism," a position characterized by distrust in human nature and trust in unbroken historical continuity.[42] In one of Pius IX's liberalizing moves, Dr. Pelegrino Rossi was, in September 1848, appointed prime minister of the Papal States. He was a casualty of the pontiff's good intentions. On November 25, 1848, Dr. Rossi was assassinated in Rome.

40. "Polémica," p. 497.
41. "Polémica," p. 501.
42. Peter Viereck, *Conservatism: From John Adams to Churchill* (Princeton: D. Van Nostrand, 1956), p. 15.

CHAPTER FOUR

Journalist

B etween 1837 and 1840, Donoso's journalistic activity mush-roomed as he began serving several periodicals as both editor and contributor. He wrote a dulling multiplicity of articles, ranging from "El Clasicismo y el Romanticismo," a collection of seven articles which appeared in *El Correo Nacional,* to short articles in *El Porvenir* and even shorter, nearly telegraphic ones for *El Piloto.* As one would expect, their quality is uneven. Some of them make all too obvious the haste in which they were written; in others there is an ill-disguised distaste for the subject at hand; still others are vehicles for a wide range of emotions. Many of them deal with topics that hold little interest for Americans today — obscure squabbles, parliamentary high jinks, tart observations on local politics, the Carlist War, tithes, and so forth — though some of these did have important and enduring ramifications. But Donoso's articles do more than just address the burning issues of the moment; often they also foreshadow his future speculations and political moves. His purpose was to influence the educated public through the written word during a period of national uncertainty and confusion. He engaged in a number of controversies, several of which became highly acerbic.

El Porvenir began publishing on June 1, 1837. Donoso was listed as

35

principal editor. Here he associated with such writers as Fernández de la Vega and Sartorius, and had the distinction of offering the poet José Zorrilla his first paid position in Madrid. Zorrilla showed his appreciation by writing an article on Rubens's Madonna.[1] Because of his haughty attitude and his political views, Donoso soon made himself unpopular with the editorial staff of *El Eco del Comercio*. They ridiculed him as "the universal master" and scored his constant invocation of the principle of intelligence, especially since he appeared to be reserving intelligence to himself and the moderates. (A parody of the day has Donoso attributing Attila's rise to power to "the sovereignty of intelligence and one million barbarians."[2])

His connection with *El Porvenir* lasted a mere three and a half months, and the periodical closed its doors fifteen days after his resignation. Nevertheless, he did contribute several articles worthy of note. Among the most interesting was his review of Victor Hugo's *Mary Stuart*, a work he said could only have appeared during an extremely sad period of history like the present one, when false philosophy had perverted ideas and customs. *Mary Stuart* is, in his judgment, an incendiary work insulting traditional monarchical beliefs. Victor Hugo is a fallen angel who fails to realize that in undermining the crown, he is preparing the way for the "leveling masses" to ravage his poetic crown. Poetry is a great force that binds men together. Donoso submits that there are two kinds of poets. There are those who are life-giving and civilizing; these should be the leaders of society, because they are "interpreters of heaven." But there are also those who receive their inspiration from the abyss, insult morality, contradict history, flourish in corrupt and impotent civilizations, and follow the whims of society like slaves. Victor Hugo, with his *Mary Stuart*, falls into this category.[3]

---

1. *Juan Donoso Cortés: Artículos Políticos en "El Porvenir" (1837)*, intro. by Federico Suárez (Pamplona: Eunsa, 1992), p. 16.

2. *Artículos . . . en "El Porvenir,"* pp. 28, 50.

3. Donoso Cortés, "Influencia política y social de 'María Tudor,' drama de Victor Hugo" [May 12, 1837], *Artículos . . . en "El Porvenir,"* pp. 158-62. Remarks on pp. 43-45.

The review was lambasted by *El Eco* as being pedantic, ridiculous, and altogether insufferable.[4] There can be little doubt that Donoso often let his political views lead him by the nose, leaving aesthetic sensitivity in the dust. He later praised the work of a mediocre playwright, Roca de Togores' *María de Molina,* just because it had a patriotic theme and included some discreet flattery of María Cristina — flattery he tried to embellish with his review.[5] In these articles there were minor errors, such as his attributing to Augustine a passage from Tertullian.[6] Donoso may already have had some kind of reputation as a prophet: he was criticized by Gallardo for predicting that if the 1812 constitution were proclaimed, Don Carlos would enter Madrid in triumph. (Oddly enough, that reputation came close to real respectability when Don Carlos appeared at the gates of Madrid in the fall of 1837.)[7]

What is the connection between ideas and events? Donoso grapples with this problem in many of his contributions to *El Porvenir.* He attacks the restoration of the 1812 Cádiz constitution on the grounds that a revival of ideas is invariably accompanied by a revival of facts: the restoration of a principle brings with it a restoration of the kind of men it represents. In a diatribe atypical of the later Donoso, he attacks this particular restoration as "terrible, reactionary, and disastrous in all its consequences." It is, he says, a case of the past invading the present and memory prevailing over reality.[8] He scores the word "restoration" as an utterance to be pronounced only with terror; it is a word of baneful augury. One need only think of the forces behind this resuscitation of the 1812 constitution: they

4. Remarks on "Influencia política," p. 45.

5. Donoso Cortés, " 'Doña María de Molina,' Drama original en cinco actos, por Don Mariano Roca de Togores" [July 28, 1837], *Artículos . . . en "El Porvenir,"* pp. 428-41.

6. Donoso Cortés, "Ministerios" [May 20, 1837], *Artículos . . . en "El Porvenir,"* p. 189.

7. "Ministerios," p. 52.

8. Donoso Cortés, "El Partido Dominante" [May 3, 1837], *Artículos . . . en "El Porvenir,"* p. 128.

are full of hatred and revenge; their intelligence is void of content; they are sepulchres.[9]

His critics at *El Eco* were right. The theme of intelligence obsessed Donoso. In what is perhaps his most interesting piece on the subject during this period, he interprets the struggle between the gods of Olympus and the Titans as a combat between intelligence and force. The Titans conquered nature but failed to scale Mount Olympus. Intelligence triumphed, and to it belongs the dominion of the world. The principle of intelligence suffices to interpret any historical period. Without it historical unity is shattered, history becomes a hieroglyphic, and the world returns to its primitive chaos. In what seems to be a heavy-handed adaptation of a major theme from *De Civitate Dei,* Donoso equates history with the ongoing account of this continuing struggle between the intelligent and the powerful.[10]

Three themes of superlative importance to Donoso are referred to time and again: patriotism, religion, and language. There are nice examples of each in his contributions to *El Porvenir.* In one issue (that of May 29, 1837), he discusses the paradox presented by two particular swords. While the sword of Boabdil, the last Muslim sovereign of Granada, is kept reverently housed by the Marqueses de Campo-Tejar, the sword of his conqueror, King Fernando, has been dismantled by the authorities for a few ounces of silverplate. This amounts to sacrilege. It is a despicable insult to the memory of the monarch who gave Spain a new scepter and humanity a new world. But this is the kind of shameful act that can occur only in periods of eclipse, when "popular glories," after the manner of morality, are forced to leave the public domain and find refuge in the home. The Marqueses de Campo-Tejar have shown themselves to be superior to the government. They honor the memory of the defeated king, while the government profanes the memory of the victorious king. Donoso chides the government officials, likening

9. "El Partido Dominante," p. 130.
10. Donoso Cortés, "Filosofía de la historia aplicada a nuestra situación política" [May 17, 1837], *Artículos . . . en "El Porvenir,"* pp. 174-78.

them to the eunuchs of a seraglio: they are characterized by ferocity without grandeur and timidity without compassion.[11]

The notion that things, no matter how precious, receive their value from their associations, not their material worth, was a constant with Donoso. In a piece reminiscent of the arguments of Abbot Suger of St. Denis, Donoso zealously defends the use of rich and precious articles for purposes of worship. His argument is simplicity itself. All nations have dedicated the very best in their coffers to the Supreme Being. It would be inappropriate not to consecrate to his service a portion of the rich gifts God has so abundantly provided. To use articles which are less valuable than those used in a rich person's household would be absurd, as well as a usurpation of God's sovereignty. Man is a physical being, and his ideas are structured by sensation, by contact with the external world. It is, therefore, very difficult for him to conceive of grandeur in humble surroundings.[12]

Donoso is familiar with the major objections launched against his argument. There are, he says, those "irreligious philosophers" who define true grandeur as poverty of heart. They would be right if man were restricted to the ethereal worship of the spirit. But man is not pure spirit. He requires the buttressing of matter, glorious matter, to elevate himself to God. The first centuries of Christianity bear this out: one need only think of the magnificent temples of Tyre, Constantinople, Jerusalem, and Antioch.[13]

Now Donoso turns to the subject of language, linking it to his interest in revolutionary change. In unsettled times, he says, disorders of the spirit produce disorders of ideas, which in turn are reflected in the actions that complement them and the words that express them. This chain reaction is evident today (1837): the ideas

11. Donoso Cortés, "Vandalismo" [June 1, 1837], *Artículos . . . en "El Porvenir,"* pp. 229-31.

12. Donoso Cortés, "Alahajas de las Iglesias" [June 2, 1838], *Artículos . . . en "El Porvenir,"* pp. 234-35.

13. "Alahajas," p. 235.

are anarchical, the actions monstrous, and the language barbarous and corrupt. He suggests that the most telling symptom of the age is the drastic transformation which has taken place in the meaning of words. There are, as it were, two counterpoised "dictionaries" corresponding to two languages: that of the people and that of the demagogues. In the first language, a word is understood in that everyday meaning which has been consecrated by tradition. In the second, the same word has different meanings, meanings not sanctioned by use and in contradiction with its traditional definition. As the testimony of humanity is rejected as absurd, there is nothing for this counterfeit language to do but to introduce disorder into the moral world.[14]

Donoso uses the word "freedom" *(libertad)* as an example — it is a term he uses often. In revolutionary eras, when people demand freedom, they are talking about what the word traditionally signifies: justice, in the fullest sense. But when demagogues use the same word, they mean something entirely different. They mean the triumph of a system, formulated a priori, condoning the breaking of all laws, the subversion of all institutions, the leveling of all obstacles, the suppression of all resistance. The "dictionary" they use belongs exclusively to them. It contains a sacred, symbolic language of initiation designed to mesmerize the people and lead them toward an attractively disguised demagogic tyranny.[15] The French Revolution is a superb example. The people demanded an end to arbitrary imprisonment, and they were given revolutionary tribunals. They demanded the suppression of monopolies, and they were given a demagogic monopoly. When they demanded the just apportioning of taxes, the demagogues responded by confiscating the goods of those who worked, and distributing the spoils to the mendicant rabble.[16]

14. Donoso Cortés, "Semejanza de voces, confusión de ideas" [July 1, 1837], *Artículos . . . en "El Porvenir,"* pp. 333-34.

15. "Semejanza," p. 334.

16. "Semejanza," p. 336.

A series of seven articles — Donoso's lengthiest treatment of one subject during this period — appeared in *El Correo Nacional* in August and September of 1838, under the title of "El Clasicismo y el Romanticismo." In Donoso's analysis, romantics consider classicists to have taken respect for authority to the extreme of servitude. Classicists, on the other hand, view romantics as having exacerbated love of independence to the point of endowing anarchy with the status of a dogma.[17] This conflict is important: literature is not an isolated phenomenon, but the reflection of an entire society, a commentary on the movement of world history. Classicism is the fruit of ancient societies; romanticism, of the modern.[18]

Greek and Roman societies were idolatrous and materialistic. Men were the slaves of the gods, and the gods were the slaves of fate. The poetry of the ancient world is rich in images used to beautify abstract but idolized "forms." Dramatic terror originates in physical combat, in external events. Great deeds are done not by individuals, but by peoples: in Greek drama, the individual is always subordinated to the chorus. Love is considered an evil, because it causes profound disturbances in the social hierarchy. Donoso cites Helen, Ulysses' siren, and other femmes fatales to prove that classical man regarded woman as the harbinger of ill fortune and a major obstacle to the performance of great and heroic deeds.[19] In a magnificent phrase, Donoso states that when Christianity came into the world, "nature was condemned to silence."[20] The theater, forum, and circus were destroyed, and their activities reduced to the minuscule arena of the family home.

With the advent of Christianity, physical force is replaced by moral force, dramatic terror becomes rooted in inner struggle, the status of women is elevated, and great deeds are accomplished by individuals. Christianity proclaims the cult of spirit and proscribes the cult

17. Donoso Cortés, "El Clasicismo y el Romanticismo," *Obras Completas de Don Juan Donoso Cortés,* ed. Juan Juretschke (Madrid: BAC, 1946), vol. 1, p. 383.
18. "El Clasicismo y el Romanticismo," p. 385.
19. "El Clasicismo y el Romanticismo," pp. 390-91, 394-95.
20. "El Clasicismo y el Romanticismo," p. 400.

of forms.[21] But a cursory look at history confirms that both schools have a claim to legitimacy: classicism, for its emphasis on the perfection of forms and the richness of its imagery; romanticism, for its profundity of ideas and its elevation of sentiment. Donoso urges a synthesis of the two, on the basis that true perfection consists in "expressing a beautiful thought by means of a beautiful form."[22]

Donoso was affiliated with *El Piloto* from 1839 to 1840. As its "political director," he was in charge of the political and doctrinal sections of the periodical.[23] During his tenure he participated in a lively controversy with *El Correo Nacional,* the periodical which had published his essay on classicism and romanticism only a short time previously. He attempted to counter the flaccid opportunism which aspired to unite the two sectors of the liberal party — the progressives and the moderates — in hopes of melding order to freedom.[24] Donoso considered any such plan ill-advised and potentially disastrous.

Of the many themes found in *El Piloto,* those of the Carlist War and the Spanish religious question were perhaps of the timeliest importance. The "Prospectus" sets the tone by excoriating the "rebel prince" whose goal is to restore reactionary despotism.[25] There should always be, says Donoso, a due proportion between intellectual and political progress. When the first outruns the second, revolution is inevitable. France in 1789 was rich in philosophy, but poor in free institutions. In Spain, however, the situation is reversed. And in Spain the only possible source of *ciencia* is the press: it is only the press that is able to discuss principles and disseminate ideas. This, therefore, is its task: to further intellectual progress until it catches up with political progress. Only the press can reform society and thus insure the salvation of the state. This is, indeed, the very purpose of *El Piloto.*[26]

21. "El Clasicismo y el Romanticismo," pp. 391-92, 399-400.

22. "El Clasicismo y el Romanticismo," p. 409.

23. *Juan Donoso Cortés: Artículos Políticos en "El Piloto"* [1839-1840], intro. by Federico Suárez (Pamplona: Eunsa, 1992), p. 39.

24. *Artículos . . . en "El Piloto,"* pp. 62-63.

25. *Artículos . . . en "El Piloto,"* p. 107.

26. *Artículos . . . en "El Piloto,"* p. 109.

Though Donoso is still determined to use the press to turn public opinion against Don Carlos, his opinion of the man seems to have mellowed. He realizes that Don Carlos's survival is predicated on his reputation as a staunch Catholic and absolute monarch and that the press played a significant part in transforming a pitiful rebellion into a glorious crusade. In a countermove, Donoso now uses the press to prove that the "rebel prince" is in fact allied to democracy and anarchy. He embroiders the theme in several articles. The manifestos of Don Carlos, he says, are anarchical, scarcely worthy of the dignity with which he is being invested.[27] Moreover, since he has extended electoral rights so indiscriminately — even to people brutalized and enslaved by poverty — Don Carlos is not an absolute monarch but rather a democratic monarch. The result is a sad state of affairs: nothing more or less than a democracy plus a king.[28] Since this hybrid eliminates all the intermediate bodies, a tyranny of either ruler or ruled will necessarily emerge: two unlimited powers cannot coexist.[29]

These observations might seem to reflect the biased view of a propagandist, but Donoso also has some rather pungent remarks to make about the Madrid camp. The foundation of constitutional monarchy — the bourgeoisie — is, he says, weak and rachitic, and so the constitutional monarchy lacks a solid foundation. Logic demands, therefore, that either the bourgeoisie be strengthened or constitutional monarchy be abandoned. The Spaniard has only two choices: Don Carlos, backed by a turbulent democracy, or Isabel, supported by a strong middle class. The progressive party has failed to lead the queen's forces to victory precisely because its "system" does not differ from that of Carlism. The monarchical party, on the other hand, has the capacity to attain victory, but has failed to do so because it has no system.[30]

27. Donoso Cortés, "Sobre los manifiestos de don Carlos" [March 6, 1839], *Artículos . . . en "El Piloto,"* pp. 137-38.

28. Donoso Cortés, "Identidad entre la monarquía carlista y la monarquía democrática" [March 19, 1839], *Artículos . . . en "El Piloto,"* p. 180.

29. "Identidad," p. 181.

30. Donoso Cortés, "La impotencia de los partidos y la coalición" [May 8, 1839], *Artículos . . . en "El Piloto,"* p. 318.

In many of the routine articles, random insights can be garnered. But there is one article — "Las Ideas y los Hechos" — which is of enduring interest, and even of special interest to late twentieth-century man, menaced as he is by the "vertical barbarian." At one time, civilized and barbarous people were separated by geography. The civilized lived in the temperate regions, and the barbarians lived in the north. But the fall of the Western Empire established a new order in which the civilized and the barbarian were mingled. The barbarians, he says, vanished from the frontiers only to settle in our own households. They are no longer at the gates of Rome; they are within Rome, at the foot of the capitol. And they are at least as dangerous within civilization as they ever were from without.[31]

In great measure, continues Donoso, it is the press that is responsible for this dangerous state of affairs. In Paris, London, and Madrid, the press is engaged in proclaiming the transmutation of all institutions and confusing the notions of justice and injustice, command and obedience, to the point of honoring terrible crimes with the names of virtue and right. Events are the realization of ideas. To be unaware of this is to condemn oneself to intellectual night; and for the press, such unawareness is absolutely unconscionable. What happened to France is a textbook example. The anarchy of ideas produced an anarchy of facts, and an anarchy of spirit was transformed into the anarchy of events.[32]

Related to this article is a contribution to *El Piloto* which approaches the problem from a different perspective: that of the evolution of slavery. In the ancient world, slavery was an institution deemed legitimate by philosophers and legislators alike. It was the product of a natural, spontaneous growth. In fact, the ideas of "father" and "master" were so intimately related that the Romans called Jupiter *pater*.[33] With the Christian era came the systematic emancipation of

31. Donoso Cortés, "Las ideas y los hechos" [May 20, 1839], *Artículos . . . en "El Piloto,"* p. 318.

32. "Las ideas y los hechos," pp. 319-20.

33. Donoso Cortés, "Los albores del socialismo," *Artículos . . . en "El Piloto,"* p. 335.

slaves, which created a new class of people: the proletariat. The proletarians of today, says Donoso, are basically just the slaves of yesterday, slaves who gained their freedom but lost the sustenance they used to be guaranteed. If this change from slavery to freedom was for the worse, then a return to slavery should be contemplated. But if it was really for the good, let us not allow the proletarians to rebel against the very society which shattered their chains.

El Correo Nacional, continues Donoso, was quite mistaken in comparing proletarianism to the higher classes of society; in so doing, it only showed its ignorance of history. To say that the proletarians have a right to complain about civilization because they have not been invited to the banquets of the rich is ludicrous; they should simply be grateful to civilization for having made them free.[34] To preach class equality is to contradict history; there has never been a society without a hierarchy of persons and classes. There is a flash of insight in Donoso's claim that "proletarianism" is the most important question which can be tackled by philosophy; he is quick to add, however, that given the unsatisfactory state of knowledge at this time, the question will be resolved only by future generations.[35]

These three years or so of journalistic activity were productive, if not spectacular. The crowning achievement is "El Clasicismo y el Romanticismo." As we have seen, Donoso wrote on a multiplicity of topics — often superbly, but at times falling victim to his penchant for exaggeration and invective, overly broad generalization, and all-too-hasty conclusions. During this period Donoso is a divided man, a split personality; especially in his articles on the press, he seems to take contradictory positions. We find tradition struggling with novelty, inherited belief struggling with enlightenment. Feelings of equity vie with political expediency. The historian attempting to view events *sub specie aeternitatis* is at war with the hard-nosed politician. Several years were to pass before these contradictions would begin to be resolved.

34. "Los albores," p. 336.
35. "Los albores," p. 337.

CHAPTER FIVE

Exile

A law concerning the organization of municipalities was ratified on July 14, 1840, sparking a controversy which became progressively more acrimonious both in the Cortes and on the streets. On September 1, 1840, the flag of revolt was hoisted in the *ayuntamiento* (town hall) of Madrid. The Queen Regent ordered General Espartero to march on Madrid, but he demurred; to some degree, he even considered the rebellion justified. So, after appointing Espartero "presidente de gobierno," María Cristina renounced the regency and fled from Valencia to France.[1]

Donoso had already (on July 27, 1840) pleaded deteriorating health and obtained permission to travel to France for the purpose of taking the waters. There he joined María Cristina, who upon arrival at Marseilles had issued to the Spanish people a manifesto most probably written by him.[2] In March 1841 she received him at Lyon and charged him with a confidential mission dealing with Espartero. Her relations with Espartero were, understandably,

---

1. Ramón Menéndez Pidal, *Historia de España,* vol. 34: *La Era Isabelina y el Sexenio Democrático* [1834-1874] (Madrid: Espasa-Calpe, 1981), pp. 54-55.

2. Edmund Schramm, *Donoso Cortés, su Vida y su Pensamiento,* trans. Ramón de la Serna (Madrid: Espasa-Calpe, 1936), p. 123.

strained; nevertheless, he did hold the master key to Spanish politics.

On the occasion of her visit to Italy, Donoso composed a poem in honor of María Cristina. It contains several passages which are prize-winning specimens of mediocre adulatory verse. (One example will suffice: "Italia, Italia, a tu angustiado seno/vuelve ya la diedad de ti adorada.") Then we have his unfinished *Historia de la Regencia de María Cristina* [1843], compared to which Burke's effusions on Marie Antoinette seem pale.[3] Toward the end of her exile, when María Cristina commissioned an album of sketches portraying the forty principal personalities of her Parisian stay, Donoso was included with such luminaries of the day as Martínez de la Rosa, Cea Bermúdez, Alcalá Galiano, O'Donnell, and General Narváez.[4]

The relationship between Donoso and this willful, ambitious, manipulative, personable, often canny, but otherwise mediocre woman remains a puzzle. Doubtless, he was a "partidario suyo apasionado e incondicional," as Schramm indicates, but the "devoción romántica" suggested by Fr. Suárez may well be an exaggeration.[5] After all, the queen was Donoso's main conduit to position and power, and he was an ambitious young man. This may well have been the strongest motive for his partisanship.

It is possible, however, that Donoso was captivated by her flamboyant personality, garnished as it was with the trappings of royalty — she was so different from his lackluster mother and his equally lackluster wife. The possibility of physical attraction cannot be ruled out either. Donoso's noted fastidiousness might seem incongruous with an attraction to a rather bovine appearance, but *de gustibus . . . !* Valverde notes that not only was María Cristina known for her beauty, but men such as Istúriz died celibate out of fidelity to this

3. *Obras Completas de Don Juan Donoso Cortés,* ed. Carlos Valverde (Madrid: BAC, 1970), vol. 1, pp. 933-1031.

4. Schramm, pp. 127-28.

5. Schramm, p. 124; Federico Suárez Verdeguer, *Introducción a Donoso Cortés* (Madrid: Rialp, 1964), p. 48.

unattainable dream.[6] Be that as it may, it is not likely that Donoso's attachment to her was based on carnal attraction. Loyalty was probably the key. Intensely loyal, Donoso had a personal fidelity that no political or even religious difference could unsettle in the least. Perhaps this characteristic, coupled with his pronounced sensitivity, found its complement in María Cristina's maternal solicitude.

But despite the veritable mountains of purple prose dedicated to the queen, and the flattering comments peppering his correspondence, Donoso was not oblivious to her less praiseworthy side. There was, for example, the time she ordered her daughter, Queen Isabel II (on whom she often inflicted verbal abuse), not to receive Donoso because of his views on the approaching royal marriage. Donoso remarks: "The Queen Mother, who does not believe in loyalty or honor, must have believed me capable of speaking to the Queen [about the proposed marriage]. . . . That would explain this otherwise inexplicable command."[7] And though he was in basic agreement with her political agenda, he had ambivalent feelings regarding the secretiveness of it. She desired the death of parliamentarianism if it was expedient and if it could be made to appear that she regretted its passing.[8] That María Cristina was politically canny is evidenced by her tour de force precipitating the fall of Bravo Murillo; but by 1852 we find Donoso complaining that she is scuttling the ship of state. Though not lacking in ability, she seems to be caught in a Hobson's choice between repression and concession — both of which will lead to her fall.[9]

In 1840, however, all this was still a dozen years into the future. Donoso was employing his Paris sojourn to advance himself politically and culturally. He was appointed to the prestigious Institute Historique (of which Royer-Collard was vice president), he acted as

6. *Obras,* vol. 1, p. 744 n. 1.

7. Donoso Cortés, "Diario de 1845-1846" [January 20, 1846], *Obras,* vol. 2, pp. 127-28.

8. Donoso Cortés, "Correspondencia con Raczynski" [December 21, 1852], *Obras,* vol. 2, p. 968.

9. "Correspondencia con Raczynski" [December 27, 1852], p. 969.

secretary to the Queen Mother, and in 1842 he contributed a series of articles to *El Heraldo*: the "Cartas de Paris." In these articles, says Valverde, Donoso often hits the mark when writing about history and politics, but makes noticeable blunders when attempting to broach theological matters.[10] Fr. Valverde's opinion is reasonable, but perhaps a bit jaundiced; his comments seem to reflect the judgment typically reserved by priests for laymen who approach theology in an unprofessional manner.

The pieces which compose the "Cartas de Paris" cover a multiplicity of topics: a sentimental tribute to the recently deceased Duke of Orleans, praise for King Louis Philippe, and an acerbic critique of the Orleans monarchy. Having risen to power by means of the July revolution, which dethroned the absolutist Charles X, the Orleans monarchy seems to have forgotten that the throne is not an offshoot of revolution but its contradiction. The king is now faced with the impossible dilemma of trying to govern a nation in which the ideas of government have all but disappeared. France is a nation in which a new government, a new society, and a new religion are daily being concocted in every Parisian household.[11] Donoso sees in France a fragmented nation lacking genuine political parties, a nation in which political faith is nearly extinguished.[12]

The "letters from Paris" are not limited, however, to a bewailing of the fate of the French. Stopping at many ports of call, they are often graced with a lighter touch than Donoso's previous works. The influence of French traditionalist thought is here present to a greater degree than in any prior work. It is reflected particularly in Donoso's lengthy discussion of war — which, surprisingly, is not marked by a serious reading of Augustine. But the most interesting sections of these articles are those dedicated to observations on the personalities of the day: Guizot, Lamartine, O'Connell, Napoleon, Talleyrand. Donoso's often acute insights and analyses reflect the

10. *Obras,* vol. 2, p. 870 n. 1.
11. Donoso Cortés, "Cartas de Paris" [July 24, 1842], *Obras,* vol. 1, pp. 871-72.
12. "Cartas de Paris" [July 31, 1842], p. 875.

enduring effect of the political turn to the right that he started taking in Madrid.

The often dense analysis of war is evidence that Donoso's thought, even at its most eccentric, never fails to contain an element of insight. The "letters from Paris," moving as they do under the shadow of De Maistre's *Soirées de Saint Pétersbourg,* illustrate his penchant for constructing pyramids of ingenious deductions. I once wrote that "his treatment of war . . . moves with dizzying speed from war as a human need to war as an eternal necessity to war as a 'divine fact.'"[13] In effect, Donoso considers war to be a universal phenomenon which begins in heaven and ends on earth. War between individuals spreads to war between nations, between races, and between man and nature. War reflects the exigencies of human nature. War per se is necessary. But particular wars may not be so, since they depend on the exercise of free will. God creates war; men create wars.[14]

Donoso insists that war invariably becomes a tool of civilization, whether by way of conquest or by way of assimilation as a consequence of defeat. It was battlefields drenched with blood that produced chivalry and courtly love, both of which were civilizing institutions. Paradoxically, war does not necessarily make life more violent and harsh; sometimes it softens and humanizes customs and usages. Though it is in itself an evil, war is the necessary condition for social progress.[15] Man is obliged to civilize himself, to perfect himself, by means of war.

Donoso's careless generalizations follow his theological tilt when he links war to the expiation of the sin of Adam. The expiation which individuals accomplish through penance and suffering, society accomplishes by means of war. Fearlessly moving into a quite

13. R. A. Herrera, "Donoso Cortés: A Second Look at Political Apocalyptic," *Continuity* 11 (1987): 64.

14. "Cartas de Paris" [August 31, 1842], *Obras,* vol. 1, pp. 892-93; [September 3, 1842], p. 895.

15. "Cartas de Paris" [September 3, 1842], pp. 897-901.

recondite area, Donoso distinguishes between two kinds of war: the war of this world and the war of hell. The first is physical; the second, spiritual and intellectual. Donoso has a word of warning for those aspiring to convert physical into spiritual combat: they are, he says, trying to exchange "the law of expiation" for "the law of death."[16] He repeatedly insists that those who withdraw from blood in civilized horror are calling a terrible punishment upon themselves. God will make them an effeminate people and send enemies to conquer and dishonor them.

Donoso now begins to tilt toward an antirationalist position. He scores China and the Asiatic peoples in general as the paradigm of effete intellectualism, recounting how, when Constantinople was falling to the Islamic armies, the central topic of discussion was whether the light of Tabor had been a created or uncreated light. Socrates is faulted for going right on with his incessant intellectualizing while Athens was engaged in struggling for its very existence. These observations end with a strange warning. Should God hear our prayers and blot out "the law of war and blood," the consequences would be disastrous. Men and devils would merge, and there would ensue a veritable marriage of heaven and hell. The earth would disappear, and the abyss alone would separate heaven from hell.[17] (Shocked by these remarks, Fr. Valverde, the latest editor of Donoso's works, adds a note stating that "this last page is among the most unfortunate coming from [his] pen."[18])

Donoso often reiterates the paradox that abolishing bloodletting only produces more abundant bloodletting. This belief, in fact, is what undergirds his defense of capital punishment. The legal abolition of the death penalty is an admonitory symptom of killing *en masse*. It removes the responsibilities and limitations which define the human being and directs mankind toward the nameless horror of the slaughterhouse. It is one of the major ironies of history that

16. "Cartas de Paris" [September 10, 1842], pp. 904-6.
17. "Cartas de Paris" [September 10, 1842], pp. 906-7.
18. *Obras,* vol. 1, p. 907 n. 18.

this sensitive man, who recoiled from cruelty though he believed in the historical necessity of war, was given a terrifying glimpse into the future and had to predict a sea of blood unleashed by the revolutionary tide.

The distinctions he made between physical and spiritual warfare, along with his opposition to discarding physical warfare in favor of spiritual warfare, undoubtedly form a significant part of Donoso's growing reaction against reason and philosophy. His theory is predicated on the commonplace of theistic philosophy that man occupies an intermediate position in reality, acting as a bridge between the physical and spiritual realms. By right, reason belongs to the spiritual realm. But it is a function of the whole human being, inasmuch as it comes about (in a truncated and imperfect form) through the medium of the body. While pure spirits (should they exist) would know by means of intuition, man knows by means of a laborious process beginning with sensation and ending with an act of the mind.

Donoso is, in effect, saying that to eliminate the physical, bodily level, or to elevate it to the spiritual level, would be to dehumanize and demonize it. He appeals to the traditional Christian belief that the angels were fixed in their loyalty after the original struggle between those for and those against God. The pure spirits are not subject to change, to the vicissitudes which physical war presupposes. Among the angels there are only two camps, and they are eternal. But Donoso seems to believe that to elevate the entire struggle to an exclusively spiritual realm would destroy contingency — and, along with it, the world. To put this in simple, practical terms, excessive preoccupation with speculation can lead to the paralysis of needful action.

Donoso had always been intrigued by Guizot, so much so that he even attempted to adapt the pattern of the "eclectic school" to Spanish specifications. The name of Guizot is found with regularity in the "Cartas de Paris"; in fact, four of the letters are dedicated to him. But though Donoso greatly admired his intellectual prowess and austere religious character, he did not endorse all of Guizot's political views; some of them, in fact, he had already discarded during his stay in Madrid. Guizot urges the coexistence of monarchy, aristocracy, and democracy, but he lacks a principle of hierarchy; and the result is indistinguishable from chaos. The guiding rule of conduct then becomes universal distrust, and authority must be muted because of the potential for abuse. Guizot was a man of one idea; he was a genius of denial. Nevertheless, Donoso remained in awe of him as a historian, an orator, and a man of clear, brilliant talent.[19]

On the other hand, Donoso was repelled by Lamartine. True, the poet had begun his career under the eye of Chateaubriand, was naturally religious, and had an enormous amount of talent. His first work, "Meditations," was considered to be a model of the elegiac genre. But two events provoked a radical transformation: the July revolution and a trip to the Orient. Lamartine turned from Catholicism to pantheism, and from monarchy to democracy. Since Donoso considered democracy just a political version of pantheism, he did not consider this double conversion coincidental.[20] In the "Cartas de Paris," he castigates the poet as a model of the cowardly, deracinated aesthete who follows the whim of the moment, attempting to concoct a religion out of the debris of past religions and a philosophy out of the debris of past philosophies. Lamartine, he says, views religion aesthetically — merely as a source of poetry, without any relation to truth. He may, in fact, be utterly devoid of real feeling, and be doing nothing more than concocting simulacra of the genuine article. In any case, because of his failings, the poet is a definite obstacle to the development of conservative and monarchical ideas.[21]

While Donoso's critiques of Guizot and Lamartine are based on an acquaintance with their lives and work, his remarks concerning O'Connell are not. Made at a distance, they are nevertheless enthusiastically laudatory. Many Catholics, Donoso among them,

19. "Cartas de Paris" [October 20, 1842], pp. 924-26.
20. "Cartas de Paris" [August 12, 1842], pp. 884-86.
21. "Cartas de Paris" [August 12, 1842], p. 888.

believed that Ireland and Poland were collective representations of the Savior. This distinction gave their representatives a special importance. And so we find O'Connell described as "an antediluvian giant," "the devil of England." His oratory, says Donoso, is comparable to Paganini's playing of the violin.[22] He is a faithful mirror of the contradictions of his people, a blend of innocence and malice, of Mephistopheles and a child. "Green Ireland! Catholic Ireland! Rejoice! In the midst of your humiliation and servitude . . . you have given birth to a king!"[23]

The "Cartas de Paris" marks the midpoint of Donoso's career. Like the prisoner in Plato's allegory of the cave, Donoso has broken loose from his shackles and rejected what he had previously accepted as reality, but he has yet to reach reality itself. The outrageous and excessively hyperbolic voice has been somewhat muted and made to serve an overarching purpose. His gift for psychological description has become more acute, and his attempts at rational analysis, though still awkward, have acquired more depth and rigor. To call Cromwell "the most hypocritical of all usurpers"[24] is trite, but his characterization of Napoleon as the suppressor of whatever cannot be absorbed by his imperial pantheism[25] probes somewhat deeper. Donoso's running analysis of Talleyrand is sharp and often witty. Far from being an intelligent, rational man, Talleyrand is the very personification of reason; he is a man devoid of passion, a man to whom other men are nothing but instruments or obstacles.[26] These are just a few indications of Donoso's growing talent for psychological portraiture, a talent which will reach its acme during his last residence in Paris as Spanish ambassador.

After an absence of over two years, Donoso returned to Spain in the fall of 1843 and was present at the Cortes of October 15, 1843. On behalf of the Queen Mother, he spoke in favor of granting

22. "Cartas de Paris" [July 31, 1842], pp. 875-76.
23. "Cartas de Paris" [July 31, 1842], p. 877.
24. "Cartas de Paris" [August 31, 1842], p. 894.
25. "Cartas de Paris" [October 8, 1842], p. 918.
26. "Cartas de Paris" [October 8, 1842], p. 919.

majority status *(mayoria de edad)* to Isabel. He gave a rhetorical but not overly extravagant speech in which he made a ringing appeal for "a child of thirteen who is an institution fourteen centuries old."[27] On November 8, 1843, Isabel was given majority status, and Donoso was given the task of inviting María Cristina to return to Spain with the grandiloquent title of Minister Plenipotentiary.

The main obstacle to the Queen Mother's return was her delicate matrimonial situation. She had married a guardsman, Don Agustín Múñoz, and the complexities attendant to such an unequal union had to be ironed out. But ironed out they were: Múñoz was made Duke of Riansares, and María Cristina returned to Spain in February 1844. The higher representatives of the moderate party, including Donoso and Narváez, went to greet her at Figueras. She entered Madrid on April 4, 1844. A few days prior to her arrival, Donoso was named private secretary to the adolescent Queen Isabel II, with a salary of 40,000 reales plus 10,000 reales for expenses.[28] On May 3, 1844, General Narváez took charge of the Spanish government.

27. Donoso Cortés, "Discurso sobre declaración de la mayoría de edad de Doña Isabel II," *Obras,* vol. 2, p. 10.
28. Schramm, p. 145.

CHAPTER SIX

Eclectic Politician

D onoso was gifted with a keen appreciation of politics and a canny instinct for the furtherance of his interests. Usually on target, he accomplished his tasks with dispatch, effectively yet quietly. No doubt the glittering surface of political life attracted him greatly, as did the opportunity to play the role of *eminence gris*. He was modern in his sense of theater, very much the actor on the stage of public life. But the urgency which characterized his political life was often in contradiction with the density encountered in his writings. His expertise was at times in conflict with the thought which preceded it and with his writings, which lagged behind. Active engagement in political life — involving, as it does, a complex multiplicity of twists and turns, agreements, and compromises — requires a certain uniformity if it is to be effective. This uniformity constitutes a deterrent to rapid change and necessarily slows the public expression of thought.

In Paris, at a distance from Spanish political life, Donoso had given free rein to his speculations. Unencumbered by practical considerations, he had veered toward a strict construction of monarchy, tradition, and Christianity. He had begun to distrust reason and discussion; he had found himself having second thoughts concerning the status of the bourgeoisie. Now he was back in Madrid, but the trend continued — at a slower pace, accompanied by hesitancies and backward glances. We see Donoso now at a halfway house. His position has yet to be defined; he is, understandably, finding it difficult to reject the ideals of his youth. It is really quite a surprising turnaround. Only seven years prior to his return to Spain, this man, who later would often be compared to a Spanish Inquisitor, had been comparing Christ to Socrates and praising him in surprisingly rationalistic terms as the most intelligent, devout, and free of men.[1]

In Madrid he is quick to endorse a representative monarchy in which the common good prevails over vested interests. In two speeches (given in January and February 1845), Donoso advocates the rehabilitation of the Church and endorses an amendment to the second article of the new constitution which would normalize the status of the clergy. In part, this is an attempt to correct the depredations of Mendizábal's anticlerical decrees of 1835. But there is more here than a defense of the Church; both speeches are also attempts to refurbish his liberal credentials. Donoso takes a middle road regarding revolution. As a revolt against legitimate authority, it is satanic. As an instrument of Providence, however, it has a positive function. Revolution reflects man, and man is a permanent contradiction.[2] Donoso follows tradition in affirming the sovereignty of the state in the secular realm and of the Church in the spiritual realm. In order to exercise this sovereignty, the Church must be an independent community, and the state should recognize its independence — out of self-interest, if nothing else. Man has always belonged to two societies, the civil and the religious; and the religious has chronological precedence.

Donoso did make some harsh, theologically motivated statements about Jews, but he had a great admiration for the people of the Old Testament and their descendants — an admiration reaching its

1. Edmund Schramm, *Donoso Cortés, su Vida y su Pensamiento,* trans. Ramón de la Serna (Madrid: Espasa-Calpe, 1936), p. 115.

2. *Obras Completas de Don Juan Donoso Cortés,* ed. Carlos Valverde (Madrid: BAC, 1970), vol. 2, pp. 95-96.

apogee in his "Discurso sobre la Biblia" (1848).[3] We know that he purchased several studies on Moses and Jewish history[4] and was an assiduous reader of the Bible. One of the best anecdotes in his "Despachos desde Paris" is the account of Metternich's lively comparison of the Austrian empire and Baron Rothschild's financial empire.[5] (Donoso had met the baron in Paris and had established cordial relations with him — so cordial, in fact, that Rothschild was one of the notables who attended Donoso's funeral at the Church of Saint-Philippe-du-Roule in Paris, on May 7, 1853.)

In "Despachos desde Paris," Donoso states that Hebrews and Spaniards are the only peoples to have been especially chosen by God. Just as Israel was a witness to the unity of God, a witness menaced by the surrounding idolatrous tribes, so Spain is a witness to the true Christian faith, a witness menaced by the surrounding Protestant nations. He urges Spaniards to emulate the staunchly faithful Jews by maintaining an uncompromising fidelity to the Christian faith, even amid the chaos of revolution.[6] But such a posture will require the active presence of the Church. As the first element of the Spanish "political trinity" — Church, throne, and people — the Church should be accorded due importance. Among other things, this means its independence must be assured. It should, therefore, be subsidized by the state.

We find here a profession of liberal faith, a hesitant swan song, a look backwards with the step ahead. A major article of liberal belief, endorsed by eclectics and bourgeoisie alike, was the paramount value of discussion as such. Discussion as the indispensable medium of access to truth is a belief at the very heart of parliamentarianism. Although Donoso will later speak of the coming of "an endlessly chattering mass," at present he is still defending the opposite view. He endorses, as an axiom of liberalism, "the principle of discussion."

3. *Obras*, vol. 2, pp. 278-300.

4. John T. Graham, *Donoso Cortés: Utopian Romanticist and Political Realist* (Columbia: University of Missouri Press, 1974), p. 127.

5. Donoso Cortés, "Despachos desde Paris," no. 46 [May 1, 1851], *Obras*, vol. 2, p. 798.

6. "Discurso sobre culto y clero," *Obras*, vol. 2, pp. 97-98.

This is nothing less than the principle of life for free societies, since "freedom is nothing other than discussion . . . even dangerous discussion."[7] But this is Donoso's last noteworthy endorsement of this principle.

In his second speech, Donoso makes two points, but they are rather divergent. On the one hand, he praises once again the via media of eclecticism; he even makes the uncharacteristic statement that any principle, no matter how worthy, is either false or dangerous when taken to its ultimate consequences.[8] (This is radically opposed to his later thought, which insists on the exhaustive unpacking of the ultimate conclusions of every principle.) On the other hand, he voices an increasing disaffection with Protestantism. A spiritual world that has always been alien and incomprehensible to him, Protestantism now seems to him a seedbed of despotism and anarchy. After all, it came about as a result of religious and social subversion. "To combat the pontiffs, they turned their kings into popes; and now, to combat the kings, they are making the people their kings."[9]

Moving away from his view of Protestantism as accomplishing the liberation of the intelligence from theology, Donoso is beginning to approximate the more somber views of the French traditionalists. De Maistre and Bonald believed that the anarchy and romanticism of the nineteenth century were caused by a process of dissolution which began in the Reformation and culminated in the French Revolution. As Carl Schmitt indicates, here is the origin of a three-headed monster: Reformation/Revolution/Romanticism.[10] Donoso will later provide a unique variation on this theme.

The marriages of Queen Isabel II and her sister, the Infanta Luisa Fernanda, as well as the domestic problems of the royal family, now required his attention. The political ramifications were extensive

---

7. "Discurso sobre culto y clero," p. 104.
8. "Discurso sobre culto y clero," p. 113.
9. "Discurso sobre culto y clero," p. 120.
10. Carl Schmitt, *Political Romanticism,* trans. Guy Oakes (Cambridge: MIT Press, 1986), p. 8.

and potentially threatening. The Queen Mother favored her younger brother, Count Trapani, as consort for Isabel II. Others preferred Don Enrique or a younger brother of his, Francisco de Asís. Some endorsed Prince Leopold of Saxe Coburg. Still others (a minority) favored the Count of Montemolín, the Carlist pretender who had inherited the succession when his father, Don Carlos, renounced the throne. A marriage between Isabel and Montemolín could have settled the dynastic rift and averted further bloodshed; but exaggerated demands on both sides squelched that project. Finally, after all the high tides of manipulation, plotting, malicious gossip, and sheer inanity subsided, when all the intrigues set in motion by foreign governments (and spearheaded by Palmerston) had run their course, two marriages took place. Luisa Fernanda married the Duke of Montpensier, the fifth son of Louis Philippe; and Queen Isabel II married her cousin, Don Francisco de Asís y Borbón.[11]

The union between Isabel and Francisco was worthy of *opéra bouffe.* The passionate, frivolous, and whimsical young queen was woefully mismatched with the fastidious and effeminate Don Francisco. Although he was duly named Captain-General of the Armies and was permitted to use the title of "Majesty," he was also called less flattering names. Palmerston dubbed him "an absolute and absolutist fool," while the general public referred to him as "Paquita."[12] Politically expedient as the marriage was, it marked the beginning of the queen's decline. The young, vibrant, even cherubic face of her early portraits soon metamorphosed into a fleshy, worn, commonplace visage.

Donoso, in the meantime, was being amply rewarded for his services to the crown. He was made Vizconde del Valle and Marqués de Valdegamas, becoming, at the age of thirty-seven, a grandee of Spain.

At about this time he contributed an overview of Spanish historians for S. A. Dunham's *The History of Spain and Portugal.* (Origi-

11. Schramm, pp. 149-50.
12. Graham, pp. 70-72.

nally published in Philadelphia, this book was later translated into Spanish; Donoso's contribution was published in the Spanish edition, which was published in Madrid.[13])

This activity, however, could not disguise the fact that Donoso had suffered a serious reverse. It had begun with the complications surrounding the royal wedding. Donoso had at first backed the Queen Mother's choice, Count Trapani. But the unpopularity of the man was so great that Donoso came to the conclusion that he would be an unwise choice — one which might lead to catastrophic results.[14] So he straddled the fence as best he could. In the end, however, he managed to offend everyone, especially the Queen Mother. We have, for example, a letter written to her husband, Don Fernando Múñoz, in which Donoso marks the dangers of the Trapani marriage and wryly asks to be informed of it a month in advance, so that he can leave Spain and run to St. Petersburg.[15]

The Queen Mother, quite predictably, forbade Isabel II to receive Donoso, and a few maudlin scenes followed. Donoso was astonished and insulted. His diary entry of January 21, 1846, records his outrage. How could a man who had served so well, so effectively, have been treated so disgracefully? He had some words with Don Fernando, who flew into incoherent rage. Donoso decided to terminate his relations with the pair and lost no time informing an intermediary of his decision.[16] Alarmed at his withdrawal, the Queen Mother reconsidered her attitude and decided to bring him back into the fold. About two months later, his new honors were officially announced.

If this clash with María Cristina was unsettling, his liberal sym-

---

13. Ramón Menéndez Pidal, *Historia de España,* vol. 34: *La Era Isabelina y el Sexenio Democrático* [1834-1874] (Madrid: Espasa-Calpe, 1981), p. cii n. 39.

14. Donoso Cortés, "Carta a M. Lavergne" [January 24, 1846], *Obras,* vol. 2, pp. 132-33.

15. Donoso Cortés, "Carta al Duque de Riansares" [undated], *Obras,* vol. 2, pp. 142-43.

16. Donoso Cortés, "Diario de 1845-1846" [January 20, 1846], *Obras,* vol. 2, pp. 127-28.

pathies — still very much present — received encouragement from an unexpected source. Giovanni Cardinal Mastai-Ferretti had been elected pope on June 16, 1846, and his first moves as Pope Pius IX appeared to be a repudiation of the authoritarian policies of his predecessor, Gregory XVI. Pius IX initiated a program of reform which generated such strong waves of liberal enthusiasm and conservative vituperation that he was often referred to as "Robespierre with a tiara." In a series of articles published in *El Faro,* Donoso enthusiastically supported the new pontiff.

The measures taken by Pope Pius IX were needed, in Donoso's opinion, to protect the independence of the Church vis-à-vis the vested interests of the European nations. The Church must, says Donoso, break away from the collective egotism of France, England, and especially Austria.[17] When the revolutionary tide engulfed Europe, the papacy did not abandon the monarchies it had formed and nurtured. As a consequence, the victorious democracies accused the Church of being retrograde, absolutist, and aristocratic. This judgment led to persecution and other great adversities. The time has arrived for this situation to be rectified; but in order for that to happen, the Church must reconquer her original freedom. This is the task that Pope Pius IX has imposed on himself.[18]

Donoso is attempting, in his own fashion, to effect an accommodation between the new and the old. Pius IX's actions sparked the embers of his liberalism — this is evidenced by Donoso's support of France over England and by his criticism of conservative Austria. Nevertheless, his evaluation of the French Revolution becomes even harsher. Consider, for example, his remarks on the two meanings of the word "freedom." Ever since his early days at Seville, when he had first tried his hand at poetry and drama, Donoso had been very much interested in the vagaries of language. Now he notes the confusion caused by the ambiguity of the word "freedom." If the pontiff hopes to succeed in his endeavors, says Donoso, it is impera-

17. Donoso Cortés, "Pio IX," *Obras,* vol. 2, pp. 218-21.
18. "Pio IX," pp. 213-14.

tive that the meaning of this word first be clarified. Christian freedom, which is generated by mutual regard between prince and people, must be clearly differentiated from revolutionary freedom, which is born of the ill-fated conjunction of philosophy and ideology. The latter is nothing more than an *instrumentum regni* — a device for acquiring power.[19]

Revolutionary freedom is anti-Christian, inasmuch as it is essentially pagan. The French Revolution was a recrudescence of paganism, including many of the nasty characteristics associated with it — characteristics which had in the past been rightly suppressed by Christianity. With the Revolution, the state began to recover the omnipotence it had lost. Reason was set up as a national god: God was deprived of scepter and throne. The ancient distinction between freeman and slave resurfaced. It follows, therefore, that the triumph of "revolutionary freedom" signifies a return to both paganism and barbarism.[20]

Pius IX was to take the same path as Donoso in reacting against reformist liberalism. Soon he became the "Pio No-No" of liberal invective, the quasi-demonic archetype of hidebound traditionalism. The year of revolutions (1848) witnessed the flight of Pope Pius to Gaeta, and the assassination of his liberal minister, Rossi. Donoso reacted energetically, inveighing against "that insensate and ferocious democracy which is without God or law."[21] In "Los sucesos de Roma," he attacks demagoguery as being the negation of all life. In the political realm, it is the negation of government; in the domestic realm, the negation of family; in the economic realm, the negation of property; in the religious realm, the negation of God; and in the moral realm, the negation of the good.[22] The Catholic world, insists Donoso, cannot consent to the pontiff's being a prisoner of the Roman masses. Without the pope there is no Church, and

19. "Pio IX," pp. 215-16.
20. "Pio IX," p. 216.
21. Donoso Cortés, "Los sucesos de Roma," *Obras,* vol. 2, p. 301.
22. "Los sucesos de Roma," p. 302.

without the Church there is only chaos. The voice of the living God, he declares, cannot be allowed to become the voice of a dozen demagogues.[23]

In the same *El Heraldo* article (November 30, 1848), Donoso calls for a radical solution — an actual decision — and he starts to make the Cassandra-like predictions which will surface full-blown, only five months later, in his "Discurso sobre la Dictadura." The background is provided by his reading of the Book of Revelation. In the last days, a vast anti-Christian empire is destined to rule the world. The Church will suffer horribly; but then, after a series of unheard-of catastrophes, God will intervene directly to save the Church and defeat "the proud one."[24] (The last five years of Donoso's life constitute a commentary on this apocalyptic theme.)

After his defense of Pius IX, Donoso wrote for Queen Isabel II a sort of introduction to the meaning of history, modeling this piece after Bossuet's *Discours sur l'histoire universelle*. One can readily imagine the exquisite torture the queen would have suffered had she actually attempted to read or even listen to the "Estudios sobre la Historia" — the serendipitous Isabel was not lured by pleasures intellectual. As Valverde observes, these *lecciones* were probably never given to the queen; and if they were, she surely showed no interest in them.[25] The last three sections of the Valverde edition (some sixteen pages) are not, as a matter of fact, without interest; but they were written several years later and are not relevant here.

In April 1848, Donoso was admitted to the Academia Española de la Lengua. After a solemn reception, attended by General Narváez and several ministers, colleagues, and friends, Donoso lectured on "The Bible as Source of Inspiration and Beauty." This time he pulled out all the stops and allowed his baroque fantasy full play, making this one of the classical models of nineteenth-century oratory; it was what Schramm calls "a sumptuous example of rhetorical

---

23. "Los sucesos de Roma," pp. 303-4.
24. "Los sucesos de Roma," p. 304.
25. Donoso Cortés, "Estudios sobre la Historia," *Obras,* vol. 2, p. 226 n. 1.

prose."[26] The lecture is a hymn to the glories of ancient Israel. The Hebrew people, begins Donoso, are the only nation that ever denied itself in favor of God; they are the only people whose very history is a hymn of praise to God.[27] Moses is to be lauded as the greatest of philosophers, founders, and poets; this is the man who shows us, unveiled, the face of God and the face of man.[28] Ancient Israel reaches the heights of poetic inspiration by magnificently exploiting the three sources of great poetry: love of God, love of woman, and love of a people.[29] But notwithstanding all this fulsome praise, the Jews remain the "deicide people," destined forever to wander, to receive from the world the same kind of treatment they afflicted on their God.[30] Few moderns have written so well as Donoso about Jerusalem the glorious, the mystical. It is to be hoped that this will be remembered once the failings of the age and his personality are forgotten.

The years 1847 and 1848 were decisive to Donoso's religious, political, and speculative development. In February 1848, revolution broke out in Paris. Louis Philippe and Guizot were replaced by the Second Republic; the bourgeois order crumbled. In March, it was Vienna's turn: Metternich fell. The Slavs rebelled against the Hungarians; Berlin became a focus of rebellion; the pope fled to Gaeta; Tsar Nicholas prepared to march. In Spain, General Narváez — in charge of the government since October 1847 — energetically squelched incipient revolts in Madrid, Barcelona, Valencia, and Seville. (He would stay in power until January 1851.) It was a landmark year. The sympathetic J. A. Hawgood describes 1848 as "the turning point at which modern history failed to turn."[31]

26. Schramm, p. 163.

27. Donoso Cortés, "Discurso sobre la Biblia," *Obras,* vol. 2, p. 283.

28. "Discurso sobre la Biblia," pp. 286-87.

29. "Discurso sobre la Biblia," pp. 293-94.

30. "Discurso sobre la Biblia," p. 299.

31. J. A. Hawgood, "Liberalism and Constitutional Developments," *The New Cambridge Modern History,* ed. J. P. T. Bury (London: Cambridge University Press, 1964), vol. 10, p. 185.

Schmitt, on the other hand, sees it as "the first symptom of a proletarian atheo-communistic movement."[32]

The four-year period from 1844 to 1848 is important in that it served as the preparation for Donoso's final, decisive turn. On his return from France, we found him attempting to reinstate his liberal credentials, with indifferent success. After a lengthy hiatus following the initial break with the Queen Mother, he regained her confidence and was on fairly good terms with Narváez. His party, the moderates, in power, he returned to public life.

Donoso's turn to the right was accelerated by the death, the previous year, of his pious, pro-Carlist brother Pedro. In a letter to the Queen Mother, he remarked that Pedro had "lived the life of the saints and died the death of the just."[33] Both of these events, the one accentuating social evil and the other revelatory of personal sanctity, prodded Donoso to define himself. This enterprise began on January 4, 1849, with his "Discourse on Dictatorship."

32. Carl Schmitt, *Interpretación Europea de Donoso Cortés* (Madrid: Rialp, 1963), pp. 35-36.

33. Donoso Cortés, "A su Majestad la Reina Madre" [July 4, 1847], *Obras,* vol. 2, pp. 184-85.

CHAPTER SEVEN

Revolution and Reaction

The horrors of 1848 must have put the pious death of Pedro into sharp relief: the mercy of God contrasted to the depravity of man. Everything was in chaos. The pope and Metternich were in flight; all the forces of order except for the tsar were in disarray; the Narváez government was under attack. De Maistre had believed that the only effective answers to revolution and the social chaos which inevitably followed would be the pope and the executioner — faith, repression, the *ancien régime*. Donoso gave his solution in his "Discourse on Dictatorship," a piece which was resolutely conservative, Christian, and Spanish. He was very much aware of the danger predicted by Heinrich Heine over a decade previously: "Should the subduing talisman, the cross, break . . . , the old stone gods will rise from a long-forgotten ruin and rub the dust of a thousand years from their eyes; and Thor, leaping to life with his giant hammer, will crush the Gothic cathedrals."[1] It was at about this time, too, that Moses Hess was speaking of Marx as giving medieval religion and politics a final push into the abyss.[2] A century

1. Cited by Peter Viereck, *Conservatism Revisited* (New York: Charles Scribner's Sons, 1950), pp. 61-62.
2. Friedrich Heer, *Europe: Mother of Revolutions,* trans. C. Kessler and J. Adcock (New York: Praeger, 1972), p. 119.

later, Carl Schmitt would affirm that Donoso gave the death blow to the progressive philosophy of history.[3] If such is the case, then the final agony began on January 4, 1849.

Donoso begins his "Discourse on Dictatorship" with the observation that law is not the foundation of society. Rather, he says, its function is to preserve society. Should it fail to do so, another means of arriving at the desired goal will have to be selected. Among the possible alternatives is dictatorship, which has the advantage of a lengthy and impressive genealogy. Athens, Rome, France, and England have each at some time been ruled by a dictatorship. To the great amusement of the gallery, Donoso adds God to the list of dictators. God, he says, acts dictatorially whenever natural law is suspended by a miracle.[4]

Donoso considers dictatorship a legitimate political option, a necessary corrective for certain exceptional situations. But it is scarcely a panacea. And it is not always the appropriate remedy for political and social ills. The French monarchy, for example, was destroyed in spite of the frenetic contortions it put itself through to adapt to the spirit of the times. The French monarchy is a pathetic example of a fossilized institution which cannot be resuscitated by either divine inspiration or human genius. The French Revolution, albeit self-destructive, was undoubtedly the instrument of a higher power. While professing liberty, equality, and fraternity — values purloined from Christianity — it succeeded in producing only monstrous caricatures of their Christian originals. Liberty was transmogrified into tyranny, democracy into a ridiculous aristo-democratic pastiche, and fraternity into fratricide. The "three truths" of the French Revolution have become the "three lies," the "three blasphemies."[5]

---

3. Carl Schmitt, *Interpretación Europea de Donoso Cortés* (Madrid: Rialp, 1963), p. 28.

4. Donoso Cortés, "Discurso sobre la Dictadura," *Obras Completas de Don Juan Donoso Cortés,* ed. Carlos Valverde (Madrid: BAC, 1970), vol. 2, p. 309.

5. "Discurso sobre la Dictadura," pp. 310-11.

Donoso rejects both the liberal principle of the natural goodness of man and its correlate, the instinctive rightness of the masses. He also rejects the ideas that poverty and tyranny are the main causes of revolution and that revolution can be prevented by reform. On the contrary, he says, an attentive consideration of history demonstrates that revolution is a malady of rich and free societies. The ancient world, in which most people were slaves, was singularly lacking in revolutions instigated by the downtrodden masses. Revolutions are, in fact, led by the wealthy and aristocratic. The root cause of revolution is not poverty or tyranny; it is the exploitation, by demagogic politicians, of the exacerbated desires of the masses.[6]

To carp about dictatorship, says Donoso, is an exercise in futility. Dictatorship is inevitable, since freedom no longer exists. Freedom has been annihilated by the demagogues; and, unlike the Savior, it will not resurrect in three days, nor in three years, nor perhaps even in three centuries. History does not ineluctably move forward. The gospel of progress is false and misleading. History — always an enigma — is at present retreating, not advancing. The world is lapsing into a new, more terrible paganism which will eventually spawn the most monstrous despotism ever experienced.[7] The reason is simple. Mankind is subject to only two restraints or controls: the inner (religion) and the outer (politics). When and to the extent that the first is diminished, the second must be augmented if society is to survive. The more religion and its mandates are interiorized and become principles of human activity, the less necessary is external restraint. But when and to the extent that religion loses its hold on human conscience, external restraint — that is, force — becomes necessary. This is presently the case.

History provides many examples. Donoso observes that the pagan

---

6. "Discurso sobre la Dictadura," p. 311. Nevertheless, regarding the 1848 revolutions, Thomas Languen indicates that the years 1846 and 1847 were probably the worst of the century in terms of want and human suffering (*The Revolution of 1848* [New York: Harper Torchbooks, 1971], p. 4).

7. "Discurso sobre la Dictadura," pp. 315-16.

societies of old, lacking inner restraint, were composed of a paradoxical mixture of tyrants and slaves. Primitive Christianity (in his somewhat romanticized view) was dominated by inner restraint and therefore did not have or need any government. However, a seed of license was sown during the age of Constantine, and the need for external sanction became evident. This seed germinated during the feudal period: a period which, inasmuch as it was vitiated by human passions, required the presence of effective government. Even so, the medieval monarchy was the weakest of governments. And now we come to the Protestant Reformation, which accomplished a religious and moral emancipation by instigating a radical lowering of inner, religious restraint.

Donoso's view of the Reformation has become not only more negative, but also more complex. The emancipation it caused engendered absolute monarchy, permanent armies, and the establishment of the police. The government now possesses "a million arms" (an army), "a million eyes" (police), and "a million ears" (the bureaucracy). It even reaches, by means of the telegraph, a simulacrum of God's ubiquity.[8] Donoso realized that the power of modern technology, as instanced by the telegraph, was being put at the service of rampaging administrative centralization; this would lead to the destruction of the intermediate bodies, all the buffers protecting individuals from direct action by the state. As the religious thermometer continues to fall, says Donoso, the situation has become precarious. When inner restraint disappears, a civilized society becomes impossible.

It was different in the ancient world — tyranny was limited by geography. In fact, the ancient world experienced only one truly grand-scale tyranny: that of Rome. The modern world, on the other hand, is not so limited. And it is precisely that lack of limits that has empowered it to give birth to a colossal, universal tyranny against which there can be little hope of effective resistance.[9] Geographical

8. "Discurso sobre la Dictadura," pp. 316-17.
9. "Discurso sobre la Dictadura," p. 319.

space has been annulled by modern communications — frontiers have been erased; distance has been obviated. Moral resistance has been voided by a Gadarene division of minds. Patriotism has been eroded. The only effective remedy would be a vigorous counteroffensive. Unfortunately, this does not seem to be possible; however, delaying actions might be attempted. Here we have two tactical options — concession or resistance — but the events of 1848 make quite clear which of these choices should be made. The apparently strong, popular, and liberal Pius IX followed the path of concession and was banished from Rome. The seemingly fragile French Republic, on the other hand, resisted and was able to defeat the "socialist menace." The question is reduced to an attractive simplicity: either resist or be destroyed.

Since freedom no longer exists, continues Donoso, a choice between freedom and dictatorship is not possible. Constitutional government is just "a lifeless skeleton," a facade enabling turbulent minorities to victimize legitimate majorities.[10] But there still is a choice: that between "the dictatorship of insurrection" and "the dictatorship of government"; the choice between dagger and saber. Faced with a choice between established authority and revolution, between order and chaos, Donoso takes his stand with established authority. Greeted with enthusiastic applause in the Cortes, this speech quickly won the plaudits of conservative Europe.

By this time, Donoso had already been appointed Spanish ambassador to Berlin. This was an unfortunate appointment. Donoso did not speak German, was unfavorably predisposed toward Prussia because of its Protestant heritage, and spent much of his time in Dresden, fleeing the plague. Nevertheless, this period marks the turning point of his life. As soon as he took office, he wrote two letters to Count Montalembert, the major voice of moderate French Catholicism, who had just written him a congratulatory letter. In these letters, Donoso argues a radical dichotomy between Christianity and philosophy. Each, he says, is a complete civilization. Each

10. "Discurso sobre la Dictadura," pp. 320-22.

claims to solve the problem of human destiny. But they are separated by an abyss. Donoso's thought is now absolutely radicalized: Catholic civilization is completely good; philosophical civilization is totally evil.[11]

Why this astonishing turn? What led Donoso to fall into the same sort of extremism he had previously criticized with such vehemence? Did his brother's death and the events of 1848 affect him to the point of transforming him into the polar opposite of an anarchist? Was this about-face caused by a too-literal reading of the *De Civitate Dei*?[12] Or was it simply the final outcome of a lengthy process of psychological and intellectual development? Only one thing is certain: Whatever the cause may have been, it was religious in its essence.

Donoso is now beginning to espouse a rather somber view of man. In this view, man is deeply damaged by the effects of original sin: his intellect is unable to discover truth, and his will is unable (without divine aid) to choose the good. Given this state of affairs, freedom of discussion ineluctably leads to error, and freedom of choice to evil. That is the reality. Philosophy, on the other hand, teaches that human nature is healthy, and that both the true and the good are within our grasp. The solution to the great social problems therefore resides in the destruction of all restraints on the exercise of reason and free will. Perfection being rooted in unlimited freedom, humanity will reach perfection only when it has broken all its shackles: its divine restraint (God), its political restraint (government), its social restraint (property), and its domestic restraint (family). Philosophical civilization, says Donoso, will triumph in this world; evil will triumph over good. In the end, however, evil will be vanquished by means of direct, personal divine intervention.[13] Donoso, well aware that the change of direction reflected

11. Donoso Cortés, "Carta al Conde de Montalembert" [May 26, 1849], *Obras,* vol. 2, pp. 324-25.

12. See my "The Great in the Small," *Augustiniana,* Annus 38 (1988), fasc. 1-4.

13. Donoso Cortés, "Carta al Conde de Montalembert" [May 26, 1849], *Obras,* vol. 2, p. 326.

in the dictatorship speech was raising some eyebrows, wrote to Montalembert that his "conversión a los buenos principios" was due to two factors: divine mercy and his study of revolutions. These had served to confirm his faith and clarify the problems at hand.[14]

His next letter is an elaboration of this second theme. The proclamation of the sovereignty of reason, writes Donoso, transformed evil from a relative, exceptional, and contingent phenomenon into a malaise that is absolute, universal, and necessary. The process began with the literary paganism of the Renaissance, which, in turn, generated the philosophical, religious, and political paganism presently active under the guise of socialism.[15]

Several letters from Berlin add progressively more emphasis and urgency to this negative assessment. Europe is dying of poison. Society is lost. Every anti-Christian word pronounced by a rationalist accelerates the process of decomposition. Because it is no longer Christian, Europe will assuredly die.[16] The greatest catastrophe in all of history is fast approaching. At this point Donoso becomes shrilly admonitory. The earth, for having harbored philosophical civilization, will be cursed. Europe will be depopulated and regress to barbarism.[17]

By this time, the "Discourse on Dictatorship" has made Donoso a major figure on the European scene. It has been applauded, excoriated, and discussed by monarchs, statesmen, politicians, intellectuals, and the general public. Attempting to clarify certain misconceptions associated with it, Donoso now states (in a letter dated April 30, 1852) that he was not proposing either dictatorship or revolution as a definitive solution. He was not engaging in speculation at all. He was simply presenting "a historical fact": namely, that to deviate from the Catholic path is to incubate revolution and

---

14. "Carta al Conde de Montalembert," pp. 327-28.

15. "Carta al Conde de Montalembert" [June 4, 1849], p. 329.

16. Donoso Cortés, "Polémica con la prensa española," *Obras,* vol. 2, p. 340; and his "Carta a Blanche-Raffin" [July 21, 1849], *Obras,* vol. 2, p. 344.

17. Donoso Cortés, "Carta a Monseñor Gaume" [August 24, 1849], *Obras,* vol. 2, p. 346.

tyranny. When nations fail to obey God's law, they are handed over to the brutality of facts.[18]

Further remarks pertinent to this theme are found in diplomatic dispatches sent later from Paris to the Spanish Foreign Office. In one of these, Donoso explores the eventuality of General Changarnier's accession to power, and he outlines a possible strategy. Since monarchy cannot arise spontaneously from a republic, a dictatorship should be established, and the dictator should be placed under obligation. In this way, the monarchists, as it were, elect their own dictator. Once this is accomplished, monarchy can be restored by the dictator. But his first step will have to be the dismantling of those institutions which are antithetical to monarchy: such institutions as the press, the national guard, and the jury system.[19] In a later dispatch, Donoso draws a parallel between monarchy and dictatorship. Both systems enjoy a unity of authority; each of them is radically opposed to revolution and anarchy, which shatter authority by handing government over, indiscriminately, to all of its members. A dictatorship may be exactly what France needs in order to save itself.[20]

Why did Donoso take such an interest in the affairs of the French, and why was he so interested in foisting a dictatorship on them? His cultural and religious sympathies notwithstanding, he understood France only imperfectly. Why was he so eager to support Louis Napoleon's coup d'état, in material as well as in ideological and diplomatic ways, when he openly scorned this "man of mystery without a secret"? Donoso did act on reason. He was convinced that as the events of 1789 had crushed the aristocracy, those of 1848 had crushed the bourgeoisie. The eclectic ideal of constitutional government — the peaceful, structured preponderance of the bourgeoisie — had been rendered impossible.

It is on this basis that Donoso declares (in that second dispatch) that

18. Donoso Cortés, "Carta al Director del *Heraldo*" [April 30, 1852], *Obras,* vol. 2, pp. 740-41.

19. Donoso Cortés, "Despacho No. 102" [June 1, 1851], *Obras,* vol. 2, p. 805.

20. Donoso Cortés, "Despacho No. 376" [October 24, 1851], p. 826.

the only effective antidote to revolutionary poison is the "dictatorship of the saber" — though he admits that this antidote is a merely provisional one.[21] France is the ideological center of Europe; therefore, it is of the essence that its extravagances be checked before they have a chance to contaminate the entire continent. And as transient a phenomenon as the "dictatorship of the saber" may be, it nevertheless remains true that dictatorship, in one form or another, can indefinitely constitute the bulwark of a holding action against the forces of chaos — that is, as long as there is anything left that is worth preserving.

Donoso both attacks the major principles of progressive rationalism and fingers the reason for its excessive optimism. Associating technical progress with moral progress creates an attractive but illusory notion of progress, a notion complementing the belief in the natural goodness of man. Donoso here and now takes a stand radically opposed to that of his bête noire Proudhon, whose ideology is consistently unpacked from the principle of the good man. Donoso's conservatism, bordering on the reactionary, will henceforth be derived consistently from the principle of the fragility, if not depravity, of fallen man. When he contemplates the grandeur and misery of man (and he does, unequivocally, affirm both), the emphasis is generally on the latter.

Donoso never ceased to hold that religion is foundational — that it is the religious domain that grounds the moral, social, and political orders. Any fracture within the religious domain is sure to result in even more severe fractures in these subsidiary orders. He does not hesitate to spell out the disasters caused by rejection of the Scripture-sanctioned model of the family, the patriarchal model. His thinking, as summarized by Schmitt, is that family dissolution and all its sequelae have one basic cause: the rejection of the theological. This rejection paralyzes all decisions "in a paradisiacal worldliness of immediate natural life and unproblematic concreteness."[22] Here

21. "Despacho No. 376," p. 827.
22. Carl Schmitt, *Political Theology,* trans. G. Schwab (Cambridge: MIT Press, 1985), p. 65.

75

we have one expression of a favorite dictum of Donoso's: Imagined paradises generate real hells.

Federico Suárez calls the "Discourse on Dictatorship" the first-fruits of Donoso's new attitude.[23] It does, indeed, mark the first clear appearance of those principles which he will later openly profess. Suárez tells us, too, that this speech was directed explicitly against those who during the first half of the century had elaborated impressive ideologies for the salvation of humankind, and had thus prepared the way for a gigantic tyranny.[24] On the national scene, the dictatorship speech made a strong case for General Narváez, who had energetically (the opposition would have said "ruthlessly") crushed the 1848 disorders. For the moment, Narváez — a gifted man, though weighted by many flaws — was able to hold the nation together despite powerful opposition.

The stay in Berlin and Dresden was uneventful to the point of tedium. Donoso disliked everything about it: the Germans themselves, their emperor, their Protestantism, and Berlin — "a city in which one sleeps."[25] But he compensated for his restricted life by an active correspondence; of particular interest was his correspondence with Count Raczynski, the Prussian ambassador to Madrid. Donoso was received by Emperor Frederick Wilhelm IV, but only once — possibly because he dared to lecture the sovereign on German politics. (Donoso thought this meeting a success, and he informed his government accordingly.) Prussia soon became the prime target of his invective and the point of departure for his black prophecies. In the correspondence of this time, we find Donoso stating flatly that Prussia was born under the sign of Satan. Its emperor, he says, is a religious zealot who imagines himself to be in direct communication with God, while his opposition believes itself to be in direct communication with Hegel. Donoso scores the German obsession with unity. Nevertheless,

23. Federico Suárez Verdeguer, *Introducción a Donoso Cortés* (Madrid: Rialp, 1964), pp. 138, 144, 146.

24. Suárez, p. 158.

25. Edmund Schramm, *Donoso Cortés, su Vida y su Pensamiento,* trans. Ramón de la Serna (Madrid: Espasa-Calpe, 1936), pp. 198-99.

he does acknowledge that the premier role in European politics has passed from France to Prussia.[26]

The extensive Raczynski correspondence, which evidences Donoso's growing interest in Russia, contains chilling examples of his radical pessimism and even catastrophism. Donoso contemplates with horror the overwhelming force of evil permeating history, the constant spreading of moral evil, the increasing impotence of mankind — even of the members of his own party — to do anything good. There is no hope.[27] In a letter from Dresden (September 17, 1849), he tells Raczynski that "a real moral illness" is attacking him, an illness which makes him view public affairs in the very darkest of colors; and he adds a bit of advice: "Don't give too much importance to my black prophecies."[28]

Donoso's prophecies are not, however, unremittingly negative. Consider, for example, his thoughts on Russia. At this time, he sees Russia as a veritable champion of conservative reaction. Donoso envisages this nation as capable of offsetting the relationship of England to Spain. In fact, Russia may manage not only to clip "the English claws," but even to stem the general revolutionary tide.[29] Russia, after all, has made surprising progress in the past four years, has a good army, boasts the best artillery in Europe, and (under favorable conditions) could launch 400,000 troops against the West. On top of all this, Russia is blessed with a leader (Tsar Nicholas) who can see things clearly and act without vacillation.[30] All this fulsome praise is, to be sure, at variance with Donoso's usual views concerning the tsar and Russia. One can only guess how much of this is related to his violent reaction against Prussia and all its works.

26. Schramm, pp. 207, 209.

27. Donoso Cortés, "Correspondencia con Raczynski" [July 8, 1849], *Obras,* vol. 2, p. 930; [September 30, 1849], p. 939; [August 27, 1849], p. 934; [August 13, 1849], p. 932.

28. "Correspondencia con Raczynski" [September 17, 1849], pp. 937-38.

29. "Correspondencia con Raczynski" [April 3, 1849], p. 923; [April 22, 1849], pp. 926-27.

30. "Correspondencia con Raczynski" [July 8, 1849], p. 930; [August 22, 1849], p. 933.

Training his sights now on Spain, Donoso makes a few remarks regarding General Narváez. The general has a praiseworthy instinct for great deeds, but his friends are a most unsavory crew. If only he were surrounded instead by good men, the general could really put his iron will and superior talents to work and save the nation. Though he and Narváez are poles apart in terms of character, taste, and judgment, Donoso has no doubt that this man is "la columna que sostiene el edificio." When Narváez leaves, the building will fall.[31] In a psychologically acute reading of the Spanish character, Donoso makes a statement which, eight decades later, will acquire the status of a prophecy:

> We have exaggerated perseverance to the point of having fought for seven centuries against the Arabs; we have exaggerated race hatred to the point of having exterminated the Jews; we have exaggerated religious feeling to the point of having invented the Inquisition. We have not as yet exaggerated socialism, but we certainly shall.[32]

Donoso left Berlin in November 1849, returned to Madrid, and then retired to Don Benito, to recover his health, in the spring of 1850. During his absence, Queen Isabel had been persuaded by two of her unsavory religious hangers-on, Padre Fulgencio and Sor Patrocinio, to force the resignation of General Narváez. She was then obliged to implore Narváez to return to power. For his part, Donoso had never wavered in his loyalty to Narváez. And so, as soon as he was once again ensconced in Madrid, he was able to resume his parliamentary career. He launched this new phase of his life with the second and most prophetic of his three major discourses, the "Discurso sobre la situación general de Europa."

31. "Correspondencia con Raczynski" [August 23, 1849]; [September 17, 1849], p. 939.
32. "Correspondencia con Raczynski" [August 23, 1849], pp. 934-35.

CHAPTER EIGHT

Diplomat and Prophet

In the "Discurso sobre la situación general de Europa," given on January 30, 1850, Donoso gave free rein to apocalyptic propheticism. The proximate cause of this veritable explosion may have been his failing health. His woeful condition had prodded his return to Spain and consequent period of recuperation at Don Benito. According to Graham, it was primarily his feverish, overexcited imagination that had caused him twice to request leave of absence during his stay in Berlin.[1] Donoso himself indicates, in a letter dated August 28, 1849, that he had been sick for several months and had feared that remaining in Prussia might cost him his life.[2] Talented though he was at exaggeration, there was probably some real foundation for his fears.

His visionary inclination had surfaced in Berlin and Dresden. There he had kept up a correspondence with the poet García Tassara. In 1841 this man had penned a poem ("To Don Juan Donoso Cortés") incorporating Donosan themes. From Berlin, Donoso wrote to García Tassara, asking him once again to prophesy in verse

1. John T. Graham, *Donoso Cortés: Utopian Romanticist and Political Realist* (Columbia: University of Missouri Press, 1974), pp. 184-85.
2. Santiago Galindo, *Donoso Cortés y su teoría política* (Badajoz, 1957), p. 109.

the death of modern European civilization and the birth of a new Middle Age. Graham tells us that the poet complied with "some disconnected stanzas . . . which he called 'Un Diablo Más.'"[3] Count Raczynski, Donoso's epistolary confidant, was disturbed and shaken by these "black prophecies." Donoso believed himself to be afflicted by a "moral disease." Graham, the only biographer who has studied this illness with care, speaks of strange, simply frightful symptoms, and suggests that this was a recurrent illness, dating from as early as 1846.[4] If what he had was indeed syphilis, as Graham suggests, the physical, moral, and psychological depredations were surely quite real and devastating.

But whatever health problems Donoso may have been suffering, his "Discurso sobre . . . Europa" speech was a tremendous success. Considered today a model of parliamentary oratory, this speech contains *in ovo* several of the major themes later developed in his most substantial work, the *Ensayo.* In this speech, Donoso's prophetic afflatus is domesticated. Having appeared in so many of his letters in the form of random flashes and unexpected explosions, here it is encountered as an integral part of the theme at hand. There are the usual nice phrases, some quite perceptive: France plummeting from being a great nation to becoming the "central club" of Europe; the members of the Frankfort Assembly talking themselves to death like whores in a tavern.[5] But this time they are apposite and merely illustrative; they do not occupy center stage.

At this time, the problem under consideration by the Cortes is an economic one. But, by attacking economics as being of only ancillary importance, Donoso moves the topic into another field. Nations, he says, are grounded on religion, not economics. To attempt to check socialism by economic reform alone is to forget that socialism is itself "an economic sect," and to fight it on its own terrain is transparently

3. Graham, p. 179. See also pp. 108-9 and 180-81.
4. Graham, pp. 302-4.
5. Donoso Cortés, "Discurso sobre la situación general de Europa," *Obras Completas de Don Juan Donoso Cortés,* ed. Carlos Valverde (Madrid: BAC, 1970), vol. 2, pp. 463-66.

poor strategy. Only Christianity — the complete opposite of revolutionary socialism — can combat it effectively.[6] Donoso is overwhelmed by the ubiquity of evil. All paths lead to perdition. All principles, all ideas, from the sublime to the ridiculous, produce the same results, lead to the same catastrophic end. And this is all because of the disappearance of the idea of authority. The malaise resides not in the governments, but in the governed.[7]

Spurred by his reading of Vico, Donoso proposes a theory of historical movement which shows how changes in theological doctrine are reflected on the level of political praxis. He begins by postulating two stages: the first, Christian; the second, revolutionary. The Christian stage is affirmative; the revolutionary, negative. Christianity makes three affirmations: God exists; God is personal; God is sovereign. These beliefs are reflected in the political order by three parallel affirmations: the king exists; the king reigns; the king governs.[8] The revolutionary, or negative, stage is marked by three negations which follow one another in a downward spiral: God reigns, but does not govern; God exists, but not as a person; God does not exist. In other words, theism is followed by deism, deism by pantheism, and pantheism by atheism. In the political realm, the first negation is translated as "The king reigns, but does not govern," which corresponds to progressive constitutional monarchy. The second negation, the identification of God with humanity, corresponds to republicanism, a system based on universal suffrage. The third negation, atheism, is paralleled by political anarchy. Then along comes Proudhon to announce, "There is no government." But for now, says Donoso, Europe is actually moving between the second and third negations, between pantheism and atheism.[9]

Veering from the theoretical to the practical, Donoso notes the place of Russia in history and provides a chilling portrait of a future

6. "Discurso sobre . . . Europa," p. 454.
7. "Discurso sobre . . . Europa," pp. 456-57.
8. "Discurso sobre . . . Europa," pp. 458-59.
9. "Discurso sobre . . . Europa," p. 460.

cataclysm. For this cataclysm to occur, three events must first take place: revolution must dissolve permanent armies; patriotism must be extinguished through socialist expropriation; and the Slavic nations must unite into a confederation under the Russian banner. Once these three events have occurred, the time will have arrived for Russia to impose God's punishment on the world. The situation is not entirely hopeless. However, the one hope there is — an intervention by England — is contingent on a most unlikely event: England's reconversion to Catholicism. In any case, the eventual Russian victory will be short-lived. The conqueror will be infected by the moribund European civilization it has conquered, and it will succumb.[10]

Donoso's radical turn has euchred him into a position approximating Manichaeism, a deviation into which he was often accused of having fallen. He now affirms that there is nothing negative about Christianity, and nothing positive about that "outer darkness," revolution. Distinguishing between civilization and culture, he states categorically that "toda civilización verdadera viene del cristianismo."[11] As far as he is concerned, even Greece and Rome constituted mere cultures and not, strictly speaking, civilizations. Christianity civilized the world by making authority inviolate, obedience holy, and sacrifice divine. Though these principles have vanished from civil society, they can still be found alive and active in two areas: the Church and the military. From this vantage point, the clergy and the army are the only true representatives of European civilization.[12] As Robert Nisbet has noted, Donoso was one of the principal thinkers to have reacted against the revolutionary conception of a quasi-totalitarian state in which all authority was to be monopolized by the government. According to Nisbet, it is Donoso who should be credited with the restoration not only of kingship but also of the guilds and other intermediate bodies.[13]

10. "Discurso sobre . . . Europa," pp. 461-63.
11. "Discurso sobre . . . Europa," p. 464.
12. "Discurso sobre . . . Europa," p. 465.
13. Robert Nisbet, *The Twilight of Authority* (New York: Oxford University Press, 1975), pp. 230-87.

In the "Discurso sobre . . . Europa," Donoso takes to extremes his recurrent theme of the impending dissolution of European civilization. He marks the heresy of the day: the subordination of the religious to the political, and the political to the economic. The world, he says, has been turned upside down. The shattering of the proper order of things has caused authority to vanish and Europe to slide ever more rapidly toward chaos. No matter how vehemently this is denied, politics must be subordinated to theology. In the tradition of the Psalmist, he asserts that God has withdrawn and mankind is only beginning to pay the penalty for its monstrous prevarication.

The speech was favorably received by Tsar Nicholas and Emperor Frederick Wilhelm, applauded by Metternich, and praised by Schelling and Ranke. Schelling was impressed by Donoso's remarks on the relation between pantheism and republicanism; Ranke was more impressed by his comparison of Christian and pagan societies. Donoso's friend Baron Meyendorff took the occasion to applaud "le Montalembert espagnol."[14]

Neither the applause nor the notoriety had died out when Donoso gave his third and final major address, "Discurso sobre la situación en España," on December 30, 1850. In this speech, he launched a vigorous attack on General Narváez — an attack which precipitated the fall of the general. Within a period of two years, Donoso and Narváez had each traveled full circle.

Some five months before this speech, in letters to the Duke of Valmy and to his friend Louis Veuillot, the director of the ultramontane *L'Univers,* Donoso had again given voice to his growing pessimism. Referring to the events focused on Pius IX, he had remarked that it was a good thing for the liberals to be called, but then he had added the proviso that they, like the Jews, should be called only once until the end times. It is well, he had said, for the Church to open her arms to all mankind, but she should not treat with

---

14. Edmund Schramm, *Donoso Cortés, su Vida y su Pensamiento,* trans. Ramón de la Serna (Madrid: Espasa-Calpe, 1936), p. 226.

disdain those who have grown old loving and serving her. He had criticized those modern clergymen who, infatuated by trendy ideologies, were rejecting the old friends of the Church and thus committing the sin of ingratitude.[15]

From Don Benito he had written that he had retired to the bosom of his family to recover his ailing health. He was reading Fray Luis de Granada, "le premier mystique du monde," and the life of St. Vincent de Paul. He castigated himself as one who had done absolutely nothing, the very model of the "homme faineant."[16] In an undated document of about the same period (the draft for a letter to be sent to several pious men), Donoso had spoken about his uncertainty regarding his true vocation — a galling problem, especially when it makes itself acutely felt only late in life, when the range of really possible choices has narrowed. With one foot in politics and the other in the cloister, what could one do? He had seen himself as having two viable options. He could remain active in the world, in a profession which would continue to feed his vanity and love of posturing; or he could retire to a life of writing, praying, and doing good works.[17] But he had made no choice. He had just let gravity prevail.

Donoso's physical exhaustion may have triggered the psychological malaise reflected in such uncharacteristic indecision and self-loathing. It is possible that he had entered into a clinical depression compounded by loneliness and teutonic gloom. In a letter to Louis Veuillot, he had spoken of being gripped by a sort of ennui, and he had rambled on and on about Spain and Spaniards. Spain had turned into a nation of fifteen million kings, sun worshipers all. Should Veuillot wish to be outside moral Europe while still living within its geographical limits, all he need do was come to Spain.

15. Donoso Cortés, "Carta al Duque de Valmy" [July 20, 1850], *Obras,* vol. 2, p. 469.

16. Donoso Cortés, "Carta a Louis Veuillot" [March 3, 1850], *Obras,* vol. 2, pp. 470-71.

17. Donoso Cortés, "Carta a personas desconocidas" [undated], *Obras,* vol. 2, pp. 477-78.

Yet he had also written that despite all defects, "the Spain of my fathers is delightful, and I feel for her an infinite love and tenderness."[18] And while he was still in Berlin, his thoughts had returned to Spain much more often than just those brief times he had spent attacking the Narváez ministry and the general himself, "le gran corrupteur."[19]

It is this ministry that is the direct target of his attacks in the "Discurso sobre la situación en España." This address shows clear signs of Donoso's general restlessness, physical and psychological disturbances, growing morbidity, and complete disenchantment with humanity. He criticizes, of course, the liberals. But he also criticizes his own party, the moderates, and begins to distance himself from them. We find themes which will reappear, more fully developed, in the *Ensayo* and the "Letter to Cardinal Fornari."

There is, for example, the idea that the primary responsibility of society is to bring about the embodiment of religious, social, and political principles, along with the realization that this goal is going to be very difficult to attain because the revolution has so drastically altered the social order.[20] To illustrate this point, Donoso draws a comparison between the Hapsburgs and the Bourbons. The Hapsburg attitude, says Donoso, is represented by Charles V, a monarch who preserved valuable religious, social, and political principles but ignored economic, material, and administrative exigencies. This dynasty had a glorious life and a miserable death. Henry IV is a fair representative of the Bourbons, for whom religion was just an *instrumentum regni* — the Bourbons, after all, came into the world just to make people grow industrious and rich and then perish at the hands of revolution.[21]

That much established, we move on to a comparison of architec-

---

18. Donoso Cortés, "Carta a Louis Veuillot" [March 22, 1850], *Obras,* vol. 2, pp. 472-73.

19. Donoso Cortés, "Carta a Louis Veuillot" [December 25, 1850], pp. 475-76.

20. Donoso Cortés, "Discurso sobre la situación de España," *Obras,* vol. 2, p. 481.

21. "Discurso sobre . . . España," p. 481.

tures, since architecture is one good index of public orthodoxy. Each period of Spanish history is symbolized by a certain type of building. Prior to the Phillips, the most representative symbol was the palace. During the reign of the Phillips, when the religious principle was elevated above the monarchical, the convent replaced the palace as symbol par excellence. During the decline of the Hapsburgs, the symbol changed again — to a sepulcher. The Escorial, observes Donoso, is palace, convent, and sepulcher combined. It is "the history, written in stone, of the Austrian monarchy."[22] The present era of Spanish history, coming as it does in the wake of the destruction of the intermediate bodies, is nicely represented by the Oriente Theater, which is dedicated explicitly to material pleasure.

Donoso is sickened by the advance of moral corruption. He describes it in such vivid terms that there can no longer be any doubt that his morbid sensitivity is on the rise. He complains that "corruption is everywhere; it enters through every pore; it is the atmosphere which envelops us, the air we breathe."[23] Yet it is still imperative that society be built on moral foundations, since "there is never a dearth of avenging angels for corrupt societies."[24] His religious fervor is also on the rise, at times approaching either saintly simplicity or sheer naïveté. For example, his conclusion to a discussion of how to arrive at the equitable distribution of wealth is simply this: Give alms!

The Church, says Donoso, has always done its best to meet the needs of the poor. But all its efforts came to nil when revolution upset the applecart. The ascending movement of the Church's efforts on behalf of the poor was not merely stalled when the Church became disenfranchised; it was put in reverse. Society is now divided into two classes which in a way mirror each other. The avarice and lack of compassion of the fortunate is matched by the resentment of the unfortunate. "Everything for the rich" is echoed by "Everything

22. "Discurso sobre . . . España," pp. 489-90.
23. "Discurso sobre . . . España," pp. 483-84.
24. "Discurso sobre . . . España," pp. 490-91.

for the poor." There is a latent war between the classes. And once it is activated by the contagion of revolutionary ideas, it will become a declared war.[25]

Gabino Tejado, Donoso's student at Caceres and later his editor, found three drafts of the "Discurso sobre . . . España." He copied those parts which he considered important, but which had not been incorporated into the final draft, presumably because Donoso had found them superfluous, poorly phrased, or imprudent. In Tejado's copy we find, among other things, some further attacks on the bourgeoisie, on journalism, and on General Narváez.

Oddly, Donoso broaches the problem of journalism with great calm. The press, he says, is in contradiction with itself. It is supposed to be the guarantor of individual and social rights. After all, journalism is grounded in freedom — in particular, freedom of speech and information. But journalism is now destroying that which it has the duty to preserve. It is now a means that is in contradiction with its end.

To begin with, the great expense of publishing prevents the great majority of Spaniards from broadcasting their thoughts. Only political parties are really free, because they have control of the press. They can easily disseminate their ideology; individuals cannot. Furthermore, the press, instead of reporting information of public importance, does everything possible to conceal such information. It is paradoxical that the institution invented to speak about public things ends up engaged in private secrets; while personal correspondence, invented to transmit domestic secrets, has become the medium providing information about public things. And while the purpose of the press is supposed to be discussion, journalism and authentic discussion are actually incompatible; for everyone is reading only the publication of his choice (which is to say, of his political persuasion) and is therefore really speaking only to himself. Journalism has devolved into an endless monologue, a party-voice forever chanting to itself, "Sanctus, Sanctus, Sanctus."[26]

25. "Discurso sobre . . . España," pp. 492-94.
26. "Discurso sobre . . . España," pp. 486-87 n. 8.

Donoso had always been ambivalent about General Narváez. He admired the man, but there were no bonds of sympathy between them; they were two quite disparate variations of the human species. The verdict on Narváez in the Tejado notes reflects this ambivalence toward him. Donoso speaks of a disastrous ministry presided over by an eminent man. He praises Narváez's military and intellectual attainments, his inspiration and genius. But Narváez is a man on the move — a man who, because he cannot stop to deliberate, is constantly being forced into improvisation. Time is his worst enemy; he is in a state of "permanent insurrection against the slowness of time."[27] And this hyperkineticism has cost him dearly. It has made him center his attention on economics, since that is where human activity and progress are most obvious. This preoccupation has removed him from those eternal verities which ground society. Narváez may be intellectually persuaded of the primary importance of the eternal principles, yet because of his singular character he is actually in touch only with economics.

The effect of the speech was dramatic. The government handily won the vote, but Narváez presented his resignation that same night. On January 9, 1851, the queen accepted his resignation, and he left for Paris the next day. Donoso resigned his post of royal counsellor. But he had, as it turns out, actually toned down his criticisms when he gave that speech. In a letter to Veuillot (December 31, 1850), we find him expressing a more acerbic view of Narváez and his government. The Narváez government, he says, has descended from a politics based on the material order to one based on material interests, and from there it has devolved into a politics of material pleasure. The Narváez government is corrupt and corrupting. Donoso does confide, however, that he is engaging in public opposition only because no other choice is left to him. He has already made several attempts to reach a solution privately, but to no avail. He describes a humiliating scene at the Cortes when not one of Narváez's ministers made any attempt to vindicate the general. It is of the utmost

27. "Discurso sobre . . . España," pp. 495-96 n. 12.

importance, concludes Donoso, for Europe to find out the reality of this man who in conservative circles has been so immoderately praised as a major bulwark against revolution.[28]

As Fr. Suárez indicates, the "Discurso sobre . . . España" was the "cannon shot" by which Donoso hoped to awaken the anesthetized Spanish political conscience. Somebody, he felt, needed to proclaim the truth: that the religious and moral degradation of the nation could lead only to socialism, the obligatory finale of philosophical civilization.[29] According to Graham, this indictment of the Narváez government was Donoso's most completely antiliberal blast.[30] It certainly was a forceful condemnation of liberalism and all its works.

After the speech, Donoso followed Narváez to Paris, where the general soon became a thorn in his side — unfortunately, just one of many. Appointed Spanish ambassador to the French Republic, Juan Donoso Cortés, the Marqués de Valdegamas, presented his credentials to President Louis Napoleon on March 27, 1851.

28. Donoso Cortés, "Carta al Director de *L'Univers*" [December 31, 1850], *Obras,* vol. 2, p. 498.

29. Federico Suárez Verdeguer, *Introducción a Donoso Cortés* (Madrid: Rialp, 1964), pp. 194-95.

30. Graham, pp. 223-24.

CHAPTER NINE

Apologist: The Essay

The *Ensayo sobre el Catolicismo, el Liberalismo y el Socialismo* is the most ambitious and the lengthiest of Donoso's works, but really it is only a modest résumé of what he was hoping to produce as his *magnum opus*. The *Ensayo* was published concurrently in 1851 in Madrid and in Paris.[1] It was on the advice of Louis Veuillot, who prepared the French edition, that Donoso produced it in a shortened form. Donoso had originally envisioned a publication in two or three volumes; but Veuillot, wishing to include the *Ensayo* in his *Bibliotheque Novelle,* persuaded him to reduce its size. The *Ensayo,* as a result, stands as a sort of untidy prolegomenon to Donoso's thought.

The book was advertised as the personal witness of a man despairing of his epoch. And that it certainly was. Schramm characterizes the *Ensayo* as "a work of combat, an eminently polemical book [that is] weak and colorless once the polemical fire abates."[2] In this work, Donoso surrenders to his religious muse and launches himself on

---

1. Donoso Cortés, "Correspondencia con Raczynski" [June 22, 1851], *Obras Completas de Don Juan Donoso Cortés,* ed. Carlos Valverde (Madrid: BAC, 1970), vol. 2, p. 943.
2. Edmund Schramm, *Donoso Cortés, su Vida y su Pensamiento,* trans. Ramón de la Serna (Madrid: Espasa-Calpe, 1936), p. 243.

the choppy waters of theological speculation. He does cover some new ground. He does add several valuable arguments and many incisive observations. Nevertheless, the work is a disappointment. It is diffuse, rambling, preachy, and not always on target. Perhaps Donoso's effort to comprehend the insane horror of his world required the construction of this cumbersome theological scaffolding. As F. D. Wilhelmsen has noted, Donoso was "guilty at times of towering exaggerations; his synthesis remained partial and flawed, in some of its details simply wrong."[3] Less significant but more galling are his hesitancies, erratic changes of pace, lengthy theological parentheses, and dense fragments of purple prose. At times the *Ensayo* appears to be an atavistic return to the works of his youth. It lacks the clipped argument, the pacing, and, above all, the economy of the three discourses. But Donoso succeeds in what may have been his principal objective: that of showing mankind, in a mirror, its own grotesque face.

In the *Ensayo,* Donoso returns to several of his favorite themes in an attempt to buttress them with more detailed, at times novel, argument. He is going to stop at some new ports of call, but first he must reiterate some familiar themes. Religion is the foundation of society; it provides the raison d'être for all other realms. Theology is the overarching "science" which includes all others and to which all social and political truths must correspond.[4] Christianity, of which Roman Catholicism is the positive expression,[5] teaches the primacy of religion and theology and is a complete system of civilization. It was Christianity that managed to transfer the notions of order and authority from the religious to the moral and political domains, thus rendering civilization possible. Obedience is mandated by the fact that all authority is rooted in God. Pride is to be

---

3. F. D. Wilhelmsen's preface to *Catholicism, Liberalism, and Socialism* [Donoso Cortés' *Ensayo sobre el Catolicismo, el Liberalismo y el Socialismo*], trans. M. V. Goddard (Albany: Preserving Christian Publications, 1989), p. xiii.

4. *Catholicism, Liberalism, and Socialism,* pp. 17-18, 20; *Obras,* vol. 2, pp. 499-500.

5. *Catholicism, Liberalism, and Socialism,* p. 57; *Obras,* vol. 2, p. 525.

condemned, especially in its most horrible manifestations, despotism and revolution.[6]

Donoso's principle of unity with diversity finds its most complete expression in the *Ensayo*. God himself is a unity who begets variety, while variety is, in self-condensation, perpetually resolved into unity.[7] God, as Trinity, is both one and family. The principle (a nineteenth-century variation on Neoplatonic conversion) extends throughout reality; it is reflected in all aspects of creation. The family, for example, is a distant echo of God: unity is represented by the father; variety, by his wife and children. And precisely because the family is structurally based on God himself, its fortunes rise and fall according to the vicissitudes of Christian civilization. The family attained its most sublime form during "the Catholic ages," in the persons of the monastic family. As Catholicism wanes, however, the bonds holding the family together become weaker and eventually disintegrate. Within only a few centuries, European civilization has declined drastically. The spiritual family of the cloister has given way to the ephemeral pseudo-family of the club — a dichotomy which reflects, however imperfectly, the abyss between eternity and the passing instant.[8]

Donoso waxes eloquent about the Catholic Church as being the only sovereign and infallible authority, the institution to which most of the positive accomplishments of European civilization — its sciences, mores, laws, and organizations — are to be credited. In an interesting twist, he traces the origin of the "principle of discussion" (fast becoming a favorite target) to an inability on the part of civil authority to discriminate between truth and error. The principle of discussion, he says, is based on two hypotheses: (1) government is not infallible; (2) discussion is infallible. The first hypothesis is quite true, but the second is false.[9] When society abandoned the Church

---

6. *Catholicism, Liberalism, and Socialism*, pp. 31, 36-37; *Obras*, vol. 2, pp. 511-12.
7. *Catholicism, Liberalism, and Socialism*, pp. 39-40, 53; *Obras*, vol. 2, pp. 513, 522-23.
8. *Catholicism, Liberalism, and Socialism*, pp. 39-40; *Obras*, vol. 2, pp. 513-14.
9. *Catholicism, Liberalism, and Socialism*, pp. 44-45; *Obras*, vol. 2, pp. 516-17.

in favor of such caricatures as the press and public assemblies, truth and error were conflated, and society plunged into the shadows. In Donoso's view, it is precisely the oft-lamented doctrinal intolerance of the Church that has saved the world from chaos. The Church has accomplished this feat simply by placing beyond controversy — beyond discussion — the primitive and sacred truths which ground society.[10]

The world, however, has now been seduced by another optic. Proclaiming autonomy, it now declares war on anyone or anything that rejects its sovereignty. It is most violently opposed to truth as such, for truth testifies to the sovereignty of God. Because of this mutiny, says Donoso, God has placed a barrier between truth and human reason; and what we are seeing now is "a secret and intimate affinity between human reason and the absurd."[11] Obsessed with their own sovereignty, people have rejected the sovereignty of God and, in so doing, have severed themselves from the truth. In worshiping the absurd, man adores his own creation. Christ should be considered to have overcome the world not by means of his holiness, teachings, and miracles, but in spite of them. Rationalism is embraced because of its obscurity and contradictions. It could not be otherwise in this shattered counterworld, this world established on the resistance of all promptings of grace. In the end, however, Christianity will prevail. Despite its possession of all the elements which on a natural level would inevitably secure its defeat, Christianity will ultimately triumph over error and evil.[12]

While paganism responds to fallen humankind's natural inclinations, Christian society responds — albeit in an imperfect way — to the exigencies of grace. When it does so successfully, it is scorned and persecuted. When, on the other hand, it weakens and lapses into paganism, it is only following the course of gravity. The Fall

---

10. *Catholicism, Liberalism, and Socialism*, pp. 47-48; *Obras*, vol. 2, pp. 518-20.
11. *Catholicism, Liberalism, and Socialism*, pp. 65-66; *Obras*, vol. 2, pp. 530-31.
12. *Catholicism, Liberalism, and Socialism*, p. 75; *Obras*, vol. 2, p. 537.

has modified creation in a radical way. Humanity has become disfigured by pride and concupiscence. The hierarchical order established by God has been sabotaged; subjection to God has been undermined. Dwelling in the midst of the universal disorder it has made, humanity goes right on generating evil by means of its power of choice. Human reason is tilted toward error, and human will toward evil. Humanity is the discordant note in the universal harmony.[13]

Donoso was fascinated by order and hierarchy. Sin was, in his view, fundamentally a lack of order: the more acute the disorder, the more serious the sin. He seems to have accepted the Christian Neoplatonic notion of hierarchy derived (with substantial modifications) from Pseudo-Denis: God → spiritual beings → material things. Any disturbance in the spiritual world, he says, will unfailingly produce parallel disturbances in the moral and physical worlds. Donoso also postulates a universal *conatus,* a striving of all beings to ascend to higher levels of reality. Physical beings strive to reach the spiritual domain; men aspire to become angels; angels want to be God.[14]

The initial disorder of Satan's fall, he says, was followed not only by the fall of Adam and Eve, but by the disruption of the entire universe. That is why the Eastern Fathers so often compared our precious physical world, subject henceforth to the depredations of original sin, to the lost sheep in the parable of the Good Shepherd. One of the worst effects of the break caused by original sin is that the natural striving of creatures to higher levels has been reversed into a libido directed toward the abyss.[15] But this motion away from God is hardly a successful escape. In a brilliant image reminiscent of Cusanus, Donoso speaks of creation as a circle of which God is both center and circumference. The most that human freedom can

13. *Catholicism, Liberalism, and Socialism,* pp. 124, 132-35; *Obras,* vol. 2, pp. 573-75.

14. *Catholicism, Liberalism, and Socialism,* pp. 134-43; *Obras,* vol. 2, pp. 575-77.

15. *Catholicism, Liberalism, and Socialism,* pp. 145-46; *Obras,* vol. 2, pp. 583-84.

do is to oscillate between the center and the circumference. Every flight from God ends in God.[16]

From the point of view of political theory, the theologically speculative portion of the *Ensayo* should be nothing more than a prologue; but this prologue constitutes nearly three-quarters of the book. Small wonder the *Ensayo* was considered by many to be a leap back to the Middle Ages. In point of fact, however, most of the major medieval thinkers, Anselm and Ockham included, would have been rather shocked by its lack of structure, paucity of rigorous argument, and frank emotionalism. Donoso was a faithful reflection of his age. He was a divided man, a man torn between past belief and present ideology, between memory and expectation. He eventually became a casualty of these tensions — but not before he left a devastating critique of his era.

The *Ensayo* includes, for example, some incisive criticisms of liberalism. At this time, the liberalism of the moderate school occupies a position straddling the fence between the old and the new. But inasmuch as it despises theology, warns Donoso, it is ignoring something no one can afford to ignore: namely, the strong connection between the divine and the human, the religious and the political. Absolutists had among them such gifted political theologians as Ximénez and Richelieu. Socialists have their "demonic theologians." Liberals? They have no theologians at all. They believe in an indolent god (a concoction of the philosophers) who has abdicated his sovereignty in favor of the bourgeoisie, now hailed as the very incarnation of reason. Believing in a god concocted by reason, they slide toward atheism. The radical-progressive element moves toward atheistic socialism, while the other factions stay trapped in a no-man's-land between Catholicism and socialism. Impotent for either good or evil, liberals have no choice but to gravitate toward one of these two extremes.[17]

16. *Catholicism, Liberalism, and Socialism,* p. 153; *Obras,* vol. 2, p. 587.

17. *Catholicism, Liberalism, and Socialism,* pp. 162-63, 166-67; *Obras,* vol. 2, pp. 592-94.

Liberalism, says Donoso, is generated by rationalism, which in his opinion is the productive cause of all error. Instead of affirming or denying, liberalism just engages in endless discussion, making ever more subtle distinctions, confusing all ideas, propagating skepticism. But discussion is the universal dissolvent. Fatal to both truth and goodness, discussion is just "the guise adopted by death when it needs to conceal itself."[18] Befuddled by the fog emitted by interminable discussion, liberalism focuses all attention on questions of politics and overlooks the far more important social and religious questions. It is trite, superficial, banal. All issues are hotly debated, with one exception: the corruption which has become ubiquitous.[19]

For the socialists, Donoso harbors a grudging admiration. They, at least, have "a system of theology." Demonic though it is, this system enables them to attack problems directly and propose decisive solutions. The socialists speculate boldly and think abstractly. They are able to enter the "labyrinth of rationalism" without losing their way, without swerving from their major tenet: that human nature is good and society is evil. Socialism simply places humanity in conflict with society and charges the good in humanity with extirpating the evil in society. Presupposing the autonomy of human reason, socialism is rationalistic, republican, and atheistic. Correspondingly, it makes three great denials: it rejects revelation, grace, and Providence. Actually, these three denials come together to constitute one great denial: the denial of any link between man and God.[20] Donoso is certain that socialism will ultimately prevail over liberalism, because it contains in a developed form those beliefs which are found in liberalism in a weak, fragmentary, and undeveloped form.

While both socialism and liberalism preach the goodness of humanity and the destruction of the established order, liberalism

18. *Catholicism, Liberalism, and Socialism,* pp. 168-70; *Obras,* vol. 2, pp. 596-98.
19. *Catholicism, Liberalism, and Socialism,* pp. 171-72, 175; *Obras,* vol. 2, pp. 599-601.
20. *Catholicism, Liberalism, and Socialism,* pp. 169, 173-74; *Obras,* vol. 2, pp. 600-601.

focuses on the political order, and socialism on the social order. The basic belief they hold in common is that mankind is struggling against evil that is imposed from without. Christianity is, of course, opposed to such a belief. It teaches that evil is personal, and that there is no way to extirpate it that does not begin with the human heart. Subversion of society or government, therefore, is foolish, superfluous, or both.[21] But a system based on belief in the uncontaminated goodness of man has no choice but to applaud all his destructive efforts and declare all the effects of revolution to be positive. All passions, for that matter, since they proceed from such an impeccable source, must be good as well; therefore, all obstacles to their exercise (such as virtue, restraint, and penal codes) should be eliminated. So we see, says Donoso, that the proximate goal of socialism is nothing less than the destruction of all religious, social, and political institutions that limit the scope of the passions, and that its ultimate aim is the creation of a new social order which will transform the earth into a garden of delights.[22]

Donoso is fully aware that the socialism of his day is a bizarre hybrid not yet wholly detached from its Christian origins. It is a semi-Catholicism, a malevolent doppelgänger of Christianity which derives its destructive energy from its source. Dogma is mutilated, Christian formulae given rationalistic meaning, to serve its ends. The apostles of the "new gospel" are charlatans who appropriate and distort the principal themes of the Christian Gospel, subjecting them to radical metamorphoses. God has condemned the socialists to be blind expositors of the authentic Gospel, says Donoso, because they dared to promulgate their "law" from a new Sinai, not a new Calvary.[23] They lust after power without its necessary precondition: suffering. That is why they are doomed to preach the eternal verities while they are trying their best to uproot them from the minds of men.

21. *Catholicism, Liberalism, and Socialism*, pp. 188-89; *Obras*, vol. 2, p. 610.

22. *Catholicism, Liberalism, and Socialism*, pp. 190-93; *Obras*, vol. 2, pp. 611, 614.

23. *Catholicism, Liberalism, and Socialism*, pp. 204-6, 272; *Obras*, vol. 2, pp. 619-21.

The last section of the *Ensayo* is basically a lengthy meditation on sin. Donoso is absolutely convinced that humanity is radically corrupted.[24] In a bizarre aside, he comments that the magnitude of the first sin finds symbolic expression in the mixture of beauty and decrepitude found in some older women, and in the eerie feeling of repugnance we get whenever we see characteristics arbitrarily joined that should be kept separate. In any case, it is only the voluntary acceptance of suffering that can change the economy of our being and thus correct, at least to some degree, the disorder of the original fault. This is the source of both heroism and equality; this is what truly unites us to one another.[25]

If the law of unity with diversity is the premier law of the universe, the law of solidarity is not far behind it. Throughout his works, Donoso mentions a number of laws and principles, but generally he does so only at random and only to make a particular point. The laws of unity with diversity and of solidarity are the only ones which remain fixed, and the only ones to which he appeals repeatedly. The law of solidarity, he says, stems from "the substantial unity of the human race and the close relationship which men have with one another."[26] It presupposes generational continuity. A man is in solidarity with the past through his ancestors, and in solidarity with the future through his descendants. His family, profession, social group — all the intermediate bodies — are the end results of a slow process of development, results which have come together to generate a human environment enabling the individual to maintain his personal integrity.[27] All societies which are free and orderly, all societies in which strength is united to moderation, are grounded on this process of sedimentation.

The last of these intermediate bodies is the family. It is the family that constitutes the most formidable obstacle to rational egalitari-

---

24. *Catholicism, Liberalism, and Socialism*, p. 209; *Obras*, vol. 2, p. 624.
25. *Catholicism, Liberalism, and Socialism*, p. 217; *Obras*, vol. 2, pp. 628-29.
26. *Catholicism, Liberalism, and Socialism*, p. 235; *Obras*, vol. 2, pp. 637-38.
27. *Catholicism, Liberalism, and Socialism*, pp. 235-36; *Obras*, vol. 2, pp. 638-39.

anism, inasmuch as it carries with it connotations of nobility, of social differences, of hierarchy. For this reason, revolution has targeted the family for destruction. Solidarity falls victim, and the mysterious link uniting present to past and future vanishes. Moreover, the destruction of the family entails the denial of property rights: witness the confiscation of Church property, the suppression of religious orders, and the abrogating of the rights of primogeniture. With the family eliminated, only the state and the individual remain. The result: the state as universal proprietor.[28]

Protestantism is another bête noire of Donoso's. He has often been accused, quite justifiably, of a deplorable lack of sensitivity to the positive aspects of Protestantism. But we must remember that Donoso followed his instincts, and that his religious, political, and aesthetic sensibilities predisposed him to reject everything about the North — its civilization, its culture, its religion. And his stay in Prussia only exacerbated his disenchantment. With de Maistre, he believed that the Reformation had signaled the beginning of the end. He saw the Reformation as having injected Christian vigor into organized disorder, and as having thus fathered revolutions — revolutions characterized by unparalleled violence because of their substantially heretical nature. The *odium theologicum* was displaced from religion to politics, while religion was exploited as the iconic facade of revolution. As a result, the French Revolution promoted a sansculottism which was a distortion of the Gospel, the revolution of 1830 witnessed the pseudo-mysticism of Saint-Simon, and 1848 saw the arrival of a socialism couched in evangelical formulas.[29]

The fundamental negation of socialism, its rejection of sin, itself breeds an entire constellation of negations regarding God, man, and society. Free will, responsibility, law, solidarity, and other essentials fall victim.[30] The progressive secularization of society, says Donoso,

---

28. *Catholicism, Liberalism, and Socialism,* pp. 241-42, 244; *Obras,* vol. 2, pp. 643-45.

29. *Catholicism, Liberalism, and Socialism,* pp. 256-57; *Obras,* vol. 2, pp. 652-53.

30. *Catholicism, Liberalism, and Socialism,* pp. 272-74; *Obras,* vol. 2, pp. 663-65.

has brought about a diminution of the severity of legal penalties and a corresponding modification of attitudes toward crime and criminals. A criminal is now assumed to be eccentric or mentally disturbed. What was formerly regarded with horror now evokes commiseration. Crime has been transmogrified into misfortune. Donoso predicts (and prediction is rare in the *Ensayo*) that one day these "unfortunates" will attain power, and then only innocence will be considered a crime. When the specious belief that the earth can be transformed into a paradise is universally accepted, "the blood will gush forth from the stones, and the earth will become a hell."[31]

But human prevarication cannot change the physical and moral laws decreed by God, who established order in the social world as well as in the physical realm. For humanity to presume to reject these laws will only make the yoke heavier.[32] Humanity requires divine aid. That is the fundamental and inescapable truth, and by now it should be more obvious than ever. That the Incarnation elevated humanity to a superior level is a truth Donoso has to accept purely on faith, his experience and opinion of humanity being so painfully negative. The coming of Christ "solves all mysteries, explains all dogmas, and fulfills all laws."[33] His praise of Catholic Christianity is lyrical. In an extravagantly phrased credo, he makes an appeal for good sense among the lower classes, virtue among the bourgeoisie, and sanctity among the eminent.[34] (Never averse to sarcasm, Donoso has assigned to each class the virtue he considers most alien to it.)

The *Ensayo* oscillates between Augustine and Proudhon, between hero and villain, saint and demon. Like Augustine, Donoso is obsessed by the problem of evil and seems to exaggerate the effects of the Fall.[35] He incorporates many aspects of *De Civitate Dei* and even goes Augustine one step further by insisting that the effects of

---

31. *Catholicism, Liberalism, and Socialism,* pp. 291-92; *Obras,* vol. 2, pp. 675-76.
32. *Catholicism, Liberalism, and Socialism,* pp. 332-35; *Obras,* vol. 2, pp. 700-702.
33. *Catholicism, Liberalism, and Socialism,* pp. 304-5; *Obras,* vol. 2, pp. 683-84.
34. *Catholicism, Liberalism, and Socialism,* pp. 321-22; *Obras,* vol. 2, p. 694.
35. *Catholicism, Liberalism, and Socialism,* pp. 285-86; *Obras,* vol. 2, pp. 671-72.

original sin prevent fallen humanity both from willing the good and from knowing the truth.[36] Proudhon, on the other hand, is the anti-Augustine. A modern Manichaean, Proudhon views the slaughterbench of world history as demonstrating the malice of God and in particular God's enmity toward humanity. In the tremendous battle between the divine Hercules and the human one, Proudhon has taken the part of man. In appropriating the principle of good and using it against God, he has embraced the principle of evil.[37] Proudhon had, as a matter of fact, moved through all the gradations of rationalist contradictions: he had been first a pantheist, then a humanist, and now he was a Manichaean. Donoso was impressed with his intellectual gifts, and for that reason was all the more horrified by his fluctuations, which Donoso considered symptomatic of the highest and most distorted personification of rationalism. In the *Ensayo,* Donoso excoriates Proudhon as a man who has sinned deeply against the Holy Spirit and against humanity, a man in the power of a demon with whom he engages in an eternal dialogue.[38]

The *Ensayo* was received with more acclaim than Donoso had expected. Prior to its publication, he had written to Gabino Tejado, predicting that the book would be universally impugned: "¿Si voy contra todos, por qué todos no han de ir contra mi?"[39] Practically overnight, however, his attitude turned into elation. Only four days after publication of the *Ensayo,* Donoso is boasting that "my book has made an explosion." Attributing the unexpected reaction to the fact that France has already experienced a frightening taste of the coming deluge, he cites an old pedagogical maxim: "La letra con sangre entra."[40]

Donoso had made an attempt to buttress the theological segments of his book by submitting it to a Benedictine of Solesmes, Dom

36. See my "Augustine: A Spiritual Centaur?" *Augustine: Mystic and Mystagogue* (New York: Peter Lang, 1994).

37. *Catholicism, Liberalism, and Socialism,* pp. 115-16; *Obras,* vol. 2, pp. 563-64.

38. *Catholicism, Liberalism, and Socialism,* pp. 265, 267; *Obras,* vol. 2, pp. 658-59.

39. Donoso Cortés, "Carta a Gabino Tejado" [May 1, 1851], *Obras,* vol. 2, p. 712.

40. Donoso Cortés, "Carta a Gabino Tejado" [June 22, 1851], p. 716.

Melchior du Lac, for review.[41] The good monk's reading was apparently cursory. Unfortunately, the exaggerations and misconceptions which were overlooked, or which defied correction, have provided an objective point of departure for both studied criticism and unjustified vituperation.

Conservatives, on the whole, acclaimed the work and its author. Metternich called it "severe and luminous."[42] However, waves of criticism were not long in coming. The harshest attacks came from liberal Catholic circles. The book became a pawn in the controversy between Bishop Dupanloup of Orleans and Veuillot's *L'Univers* — that is, between the liberal and conservative wings of French Catholicism. Abbé Gaduel, backed by Dupanloup, launched a harsh attack against the work and its author. This was to have serious repercussions in the immediate future. It embroiled Donoso in a struggle which would bolt national borders and land in Rome, in the hands of Pope Pius IX.

The *Ensayo* has provided a point of departure for controversy ever since its simultaneous publication in Madrid and Paris in 1851. Perhaps Fr. Suárez is correct in believing that Donoso was attempting to connect theology to life so as to prove that a world separated from God is metaphysically impossible. Beyond doubt, the *Ensayo* was a gauntlet thrown in the face of political orthodoxy.[43] Much of its later misinterpretation stems from its having been taken as a theological work in the strict sense. It is decidedly not that. But the *Ensayo* is, in its own idiosyncratic way, theological. Donoso believed it to be so; indeed, his principles required that it be so. For above all else, he was concerned with driving home the point that the political and social domains find their ground and explanation in the religious domain. We are dealing here with nothing less than a nineteenth-century reduction of the arts to theology.

41. Donoso Cortés, "Carta al Director de *L'Univers*" [March 3, 1851], *Obras,* vol. 2, p. 703.

42. *Obras,* vol. 2, p. 706 n. 1.

43. Federico Suárez Verdeguer, *Introducción a Donoso Cortés* (Madrid: Rialp, 1964), pp. 199-200, 207-10.

CHAPTER TEN

Diplomat and Apostle

Donoso's years as ambassador to France (1851-1853) were his last. They were eventful, tragic, and touched by adventure. Whereas his relationship with Emperor Frederick Wilhelm had included only one official interview, he was received often by Napoleon III, both officially and unofficially, and actually became a confidant of the president/emperor. According to Graham, although Empress Eugénie's first impressions were not favorable, she came to love him and confide in him as well.[1] Donoso moved within the highest circles of French society and frequented the legitimist salons of Faubourg Saint-Germain.[2]

The initial friendship with Louis Napoleon weakened, however, when it became clear that a real unity of thought and purpose between them was impossible. Louis Napoleon was basically a liberal — one who had remained religious in an ectoplasmic sense, having distilled the religion of his ancestors down to something close to romantic humanitarianism.[3] He occupied a position somewhere

1. John T. Graham, *Donoso Cortés: Utopian Romanticist and Political Realist* (Columbia: University of Missouri, 1974), p. 193.

2. Edmund Schramm, *Donoso Cortés, su Vida y su Pensamiento,* trans. Ramón de la Serna (Madrid: Espasa-Calpe, 1936), pp. 314-15.

3. Albert Guerard, *Napoleon III* (Cambridge: Harvard University Press, 1943), pp. 57-58.

between Donoso and Lamennais, a major figure of French liberal Catholicism who, because of his questionable zeal in the service of the poor, was eventually defrocked. Revolutionary enthusiasm was rife: 1848 was dubbed "the mad and holy year."[4] The emperor-to-be was extremely superstitious, both in trivial ways and in his all-embracing faith in Napoleon as the prophet of a new order.[5] He cannily exploited Louis Philippe's self-destructive propagation of the Napoleonic legend, turning it to his own benefit. In 1848 he was elected president of the republic, and in 1852 he was proclaimed emperor.

Donoso advised in favor of Louis Napoleon's coup d'état and probably helped to finance it. When the empire was proclaimed on December 2, 1852, he welcomed it for the same reason that Marx excoriated it: the prospect of rule by the saber and the cowl. Donoso helped the emperor to obtain international recognition — a difficult task in light of the fact that Russia and Prussia had refused to recognize the empire. He represented Queen Isabel II at the marriage of the emperor with the Condesa de Tebas, Eugenia de Montijo, and probably took part in some of the conservative plots being hatched toward a permanent reversal of the revolutionary tide. There is reason to believe that Empress Eugénie contemplated the possibility of uniting the Catholic powers (France, Austria, Bavaria, Spain, and Spanish America), and that this was the agenda behind the adventure in Mexico which transformed that country into an empire ruled by an Austrian archduke.[6] Though this might seem a rather farfetched speculation, it is known that at about this time Napoleon III was contemplating some rather adventurous projects. Donoso writes, for example, of his own misgivings upon hearing reports that the emperor had contracted for a fleet of steamers,

4. Guerard, p. 60.

5. Guerard, p. 38. It should be noted, however, that Guerard has Napoleon III borrowing money from "the Spanish ambassador Marshal Narváez" (p. 131). Donoso was the ambassador at the time; Narváez was in Paris too, but in exile.

6. Carl Schmitt, *Interpretación Europea de Donoso Cortés* (Madrid: Rialp, 1963), pp. 126-27.

convertible to military use, to be based at Cherbourg.[7] In any case, he soon became disenchanted with Louis Napoleon and predicted, in early 1853, the participants and scenario of the Crimean War.[8]

At this time Donoso's religious life gained in profundity, and its outward manifestations multiplied. He wore hair shirts, made pilgrimages, cooperated with the Society of St. Vincent de Paul, visited the poor and imprisoned, made substantial donations, and heightened his devotional practices. Donoso was now able to model his life after those ascetic saints he most admired. With only a touch of irony, the Austrian ambassador at Paris, Count Hübner, referred to him as the "apôtre prêchant aus sauvages des salon."[9] Within the gilded cocoon of the Spanish embassy and the formal dress of an ambassador, a Spanish ascetic was being formed.

Louis Napoleon fascinated him. Kind, astute, bizarre, and vindictive, the emperor harbored ambitions of revenging Waterloo by invading England. The "man of mystery without a secret," the "sphinx without a riddle" was obsessed by a vision of a democratic empire ruled by a crowned dictator. His disconcerting idiosyncrasies and restless imagination intrigued the Spaniard, as did his guile and remarkable adroitness. Donoso characterized him as a mixture of Machiavelli and the Borgias, "a man of which everything can be feared."[10] He was, indeed, a man of incompatible qualities, a strange blend of practical ability with pseudo-mystical exaltation. This man, who doted on coincidences, observed fortunate and unfortunate days, and acted decisively on glorious anniversaries, possessed the most complex and the oddest nature Donoso had ever encountered.[11]

7. Donoso Cortés, "Despacho No. 45" [January 25, 1853], *Obras Completas de Don Juan Donoso Cortés,* ed. Carlos Valverde (Madrid: BAC, 1970), vol. 2, p. 903.

8. Graham, pp. 214-15.

9. Schramm, p. 332.

10. Donoso Cortés, "Despacho No. 675" [October 21, 1852], *Obras,* vol. 2, p. 887; and "Despacho No. 14" [January 10, 1853], p. 896.

11. Donoso Cortés, "Despacho No. 45" [January 25, 1853], *Obras,* vol. 2, pp. 901-2.

Donoso's observations are not, however, limited to the French scene. He pictures Tsar Nicholas as considering himself the legitimate heir of the Byzantine emperors, lusting after Constantinople, and being the only statesman in Europe whose principal objective is to combat the revolution.[12] When he visits Metternich at Brussels, he sees him as a majestic ruin of another age, the personification of good sense. In a perceptive aside, Donoso places Metternich, for decades the arbiter of conservative Europe, among those persons who reach the heights, not through natural genius, but by means of observation and the diligent study of minutiae.[13]

Donoso's gift for psychological analysis has matured. His pictures have become sharper, more focused, less exaggerated. Drawn with a light hand, unforced, the images are now integral to his exposition. Rhetorical flourish and fustian are still present, but to a lesser degree. Although one does find glaring exceptions, they are rare and seldom destructive of the movement of his thought.

Donoso spent the last few years of his life engaging in fierce controversy with liberal French Catholics while struggling against the ravages of a terminal disease. In a series of letters culminating in a minor treatise (the letter to Cardinal Fornari), he strives to express himself more compactly and less pedantically. A letter written in June 1851 to his friend Gabino Tejado reflects a chastened and humbled Donoso. In this letter he attacks the individual "yo," the self, as satanic and antisocial. "Yo," he says, is the only pronoun in hell; the "yo" is the mirror of its cold and wild pride. Those societies in which the pronoun "yo" is much used and abused are societies in decline. Egotism is destructive. Societies willing to forget the "yo" will be certain to ascend. Donoso castigates what he considers a typically Spanish vice, a perpetually resounding "yo."[14]

---

12. Donoso Cortés, "Despacho No. 129" [February 24, 1852], *Obras,* vol. 2, p. 854; "Despacho No. 208" [March 24, 1853], p. 912.

13. Donoso Cortés, "Despacho No. 46" [May 1, 1951], *Obras,* vol. 2, pp. 796, 799; "Carta a Raczynski" [May 9, 1851], p. 912.

14. Donoso Cortés, "Carta al Director de *El Orden*" [June 10, 1851], *Obras,* vol. 2, pp. 720-21.

There have been several epochs, says Donoso, in which the world has suffered from intellectual and moral strabismus. In such eras, everything is seen in a distorted manner. For example, "someone" (Proudhon) has actually stated that property is theft. The day is coming when the lie will proclaim itself the truth and society will be unable to tell which is which. It will, like Pilate, ask from the curial seat, "What is truth?" But the world will not receive an answer until a blast of light radiates through this darkest of nights.[15] (End-time scenarios have always fascinated Donoso, and they will do so until the end of his life. The Book of Revelation was the model for many of his predictions.)

Notwithstanding his apocalyptic inclinations and his reiterated attacks on liberalism and rationalism, Donoso was not blind to the demands of social justice. In a letter to María Cristina (possibly a conflation of two letters — one to the Queen, the other to the Queen Mother[16]), he insists that Europe is suffering from a great epidemic: the universal insurrection of the hungry against the surfeited. This insurrection has come about because the rich have lost the virtue of charity and the poor have lost the virtue of patience. And the poor will never be patient if the rich do not first practice charity.

This simultaneous loss of two Christian virtues has caused the violent upheavals which are plaguing the world. Citing the unhappy experience of Louis Philippe, Donoso calls upon rulers to set the example. It is imperative that riches be distributed justly. Instead of luxurious celebrations for the rich, there should be substantial alms for the poor. Riches accumulated through massive egotism should be distributed on a massive scale. Adding incentive to an admonition he must have felt would otherwise pass unnoticed, Donoso points out that since the poor are the special friends of God, he will surely not permit a crown which befriends the poor to get toppled.[17]

---

15. "Carta al Director de *El Orden*," pp. 720-21.

16. See Valverde's remarks, *Obras*, vol. 2, p. 722 n. 1.

17. Donoso Cortés, "Carta a María Cristina" [undated], *Obras*, vol. 2, pp. 724-26.

Returning to the religious domain, Donoso faults the revolution for dislodging the Catholic spirit from Spanish political and economic legislation. This presence must be restored. The Church must be allowed to fulfill her teaching mission — a mission which has been usurped by "obscure journalists and ignorant charlatans."[18] The Word, once it is separated from the Church, becomes a vehicle of perdition. Every society which apostatizes from Catholicism is inevitably subverted by socialism. Spain will either return to Catholicism or become completely socialist.[19] Once again, the emphasis is on the intimate connection between the religious and the political.

El Heraldo, a liberal newspaper, had cited Donoso as still holding views which he had long since discarded. Wishing to set the record straight, he proceeds to give what amounts to a summary of the *Ensayo.* He attacks the ideology of *El Heraldo* and, of course, takes aim at all his usual bugbears: rationalism, liberalism, parliamentarianism, discussion, and "human rights." He first clears the deck by contrasting God as "the distillate of right" with man as "the distillate of duty." From there he goes on to discuss parliamentarianism as "the negation of government," liberalism as "the negation of freedom," and rationalism as "the affirmation of insanity."[20] It is only when both rulers and subjects are mindful of God's commandments that there can be social well-being, a state of real freedom reflecting proper disposition in the organism of all its parts.

Donoso interrupts his usual savaging of discussion to make the point that he is not against all discussion. He is inimical only to one kind of discussion: the kind which usurps God's authority by setting itself up as the ultimate criterion of truth. It should be obvious that he is not against discussion as such; everyone knows, for example, of his great interest in the writings of the Fathers and Doctors of the Church, and how much discussion is involved in those writings.

---

18. "Carta a María Cristina," p. 727.
19. "Carta a María Cristina," p. 728.
20. Donoso Cortés, "Carta al Director de *El Heraldo*" [April 15, 1852], *Obras,* vol. 2, pp. 735-36.

Nevertheless, discussion should be avoided as much as possible, since it so easily degenerates into the kind of dispute that blunts charity and inflames the passions.[21] And though he does oppose parliamentarianism, which is a false doctrine, he does not oppose the parliament itself, which is an indifferent form. But though he concedes that tyrannies and revolutions may have some positive effects, he neither approves of them nor attempts to provide any justification for them. He states simply that both situations occur in accordance with a law of the moral world: "When societies do not obey God's law, they are handed over to the brutality of facts."[22] To destroy the dikes of tradition and to base society on discussion is to set the Furies loose on society.

The "Carta al Cardenal Fornari," Donoso's last work, is a sort of prize essay. Cardinal Fornari had met Donoso when he was nuncio to France. Later appointed Prefect of the Sacred Congregation of Studies, he wrote to Donoso, in May 1852, a letter on behalf of Pope Pius IX. Accompanying this letter was a document, entitled *Syllabus eorum quae in colligendis notanalisque eroribus ab oculos haberi possunt,* which consisted of twenty-eight chapters on the principal theological and philosophical errors of the day.[23] Donoso was asked to respond, and he did so with his letter to Cardinal Fornari. Much of this letter would be incorporated into the "Syllabus of Errors" which accompanied the pontiff's encyclical *Quanta Cura.* (When the encyclical was promulgated on December 8, 1864, Donoso had been dead for over eleven years. Napoleon III treated the "Syllabus" as seditious and forbade its publication in France.)

The letter to Fornari begins with a terse restatement of one of Donoso's constant themes. Every contemporary error, says Donoso, can be reduced to a heresy. And every modern heresy can be reduced to an ancient heresy already condemned by the Church. What distinguishes the present age is its "satanic audacity" in inculcating

21. "Carta al Director de *El Heraldo*" [April 30, 1852], p. 739.
22. "Carta al Director de *El Heraldo*," pp. 740-41.
23. Valverde's introduction, *Obras,* vol. 1, p. 73.

these ancient errors into society to such a point that each heresy seems to produce a revolution.[24] Theological error has been injected into the social and political domains. Errors described in ancient tomes have passed into current periodicals, institutions, laws — they are everywhere.

Actually, continues Donoso, the great number of contemporary errors can be reduced to two supreme negations: the denial of Providence and the denial of sin. These two errors generate all the rest. And ultimately all of the many negations can be reduced to one: the denial of the "sovereign dogma" of the Holy Trinity, which is the touchstone of the Christian faith and the foundation of all dogma. Rejection of this cornerstone is the origin of a vast naturalistic system which is the radical contradiction of Christianity.[25] This anti-Christianity affirms that humankind is naturally good, that human reason is autonomous, and that progress is made through discussion. It enshrines discussion as the criterion of truth and error. Hence such sacred cows as freedom of the press, the inviolability of parliament, and the sovereignty of deliberative assemblies.[26]

The Church is imprisoned in the sanctuary, God in heaven, and those principles which have heretofore constituted society are either rejected or diluted, all to the purpose of transforming this valley of tears into a garden of delights.[27] Socialists disseminate the infection by advocating atheism: denial of the origin of authority leads to the denial of all authority, either social or political, just as the denial of divine paternity leads to the negation of the patriarchal family. God can be denied outright. But it is also possible to deny God indirectly, by equating him with all of reality. Political pantheism is democracy; God is redefined as the masses. The individual becomes a mere atom within a totality, and the totality becomes the new divinity. This new divinity, however, is graced with only one attribute: omnipotence.

24. "Carta al Cardenal Fornari" [June 19, 1852], *Obras,* vol. 2, pp. 744-45.
25. "Carta al Cardenal Fornari," pp. 746-47.
26. "Carta al Cardenal Fornari," p. 749.
27. "Carta al Cardenal Fornari," p. 753.

Donoso sees on the horizon the advent of a "colossal demagogic empire," led by a plebeian of satanic grandeur: the "man of sin" prophesied by St. Paul.[28]

Three principal errors have joined to produce the present chaos. First, there is the sovereignty of human reason, which in the political order becomes the sovereignty of intelligence. Then there is the natural rectitude of the human will, which translates to a social egalitarianism expressed by a republican system of government mandating universal suffrage. Finally, there is the justification of all human appetites as such: the ultimate goal of government becomes the satisfaction of all concupiscences. The Church itself is under attack from these errors. It must defend itself against attempts to corrode its unity by turning the papacy into a turbulent aristocracy under the guise of collegiality, and against the principle of the sovereignty of the masses, which would divide the papacy into shattered fragments. In spite of these dangers, Donoso believes the Church will perdure.[29]

From another perspective, the cause of all the depredations of modernity is an ignoring of, or an attempt to distort, the immutable hierarchical order placed by God at the heart of nature — the superiority of the supernatural to the natural, of faith to reason, of grace to free will, of Providence to freedom, of church to state — an order reflecting the basic hierarchical fact, that of the superiority of God to man. If society is to be saved, this order must be restored; and this is the task of the Church. To carry out this task, the Church can allow or even promote freedom in certain areas, but freedom cannot constitute its major goal. The Church cannot, for example, accept the principle of freedom of education, since this principle implies that truth has yet to be discovered and can be arrived at only through the prolonged discussion of all possible opinions.[30]

This polemic, which flew in the face of public orthodoxy, took place against the background of the internecine struggles of French Cathol-

28. "Carta al Cardenal Fornari," pp. 754-55.
29. "Carta al Cardenal Fornari," pp. 756-57.
30. "Carta al Cardenal Fornari," p. 761.

icism. Pius IX recommended the position advocated by Bishop Dupanloup and Montalembert regarding the Falloux Law;[31] later, however, he came out in support of Veuillot's *L'Univers* and Donoso. In the
interim, Abbé Gaduel published (in *Ami de la Religion*) a series of
aggressively critical pieces against the *Ensayo*. Archbishop Sibour of
Paris had (on February 17, 1853) issued an order forbidding his clergy
and laity to read *L'Univers;* nevertheless, he had Gaduel's charges
against Donoso removed from the diocesan records.[32]

On February 24, 1853, in a letter to Pius IX, Donoso struck back.
Scoring Gaduel for his woeful lack of civility, attacking Dupanloup
as "a turbulent and bellicose prelate," and criticizing Sibour's condemnation of *L'Univers,* Donoso defended himself energetically
against his detractors. Once again, he pointed to the dangers of
Gallicanism and democracy for the Church, even chiding "journalistic prelates" who were debasing their episcopal dignity by debating
instead of teaching, by fanning the flames of passion instead of
silencing them.[33] The pope responded by praising Donoso's work.
In an article reputedly written by the Jesuit father Taparelli, the
Vatican publication *Civiltà Cattolica* praised the *Ensayo* while cast-
ing an admonitory eye on the author's exaggerations.[34]

In Paris, Donoso was plagued with a number of galling problems.
The confiscations of Napoleon III's government against the Orleans
family extended to the Duke of Montpensier, the husband of the
queen's sister, the Infanta Luisa Fernanda. Donoso wrote to Turgot,
Minister of Foreign Affairs, on behalf of Montpensier; at the same
time, he gently advised the duke to remember that he was now a
Spanish dignitary and should therefore keep a certain distance from
French politics.[35] Donoso was also pestered by General Narváez.

31. "Carta al Cardenal Fornari," p. 761 n. 1.

32. Graham, pp. 297-99.

33. Donoso Cortés, "Carta a su santidad Pio IX" [undated], *Obras,* vol. 2, pp.
973-79.

34. Graham, pp. 299-300.

35. Donoso Cortés, "Carta al Marqués de Turgot" [undated], *Obras,* vol. 2, pp.
733-35; "Carta al Duque de Montpensier" [March 29, 1852], pp. 731-32.

On one occasion, Narváez obtained a passport from him under ambiguous circumstances — with, of course, profuse protestations of good faith. Sor Patrocinio, the hallucinatory nun, arrived at the embassy after having escaped from a convent in Rome. Though she wanted to return to Spain, Donoso persuaded her to enter a convent in Montpellier.

Controversy pursued him to the end. In an article published by *Revue des deux mondes,* Albert de Broglie placed Ventura, Msgr. Gaume, and Donoso together as defenders of the Catholicism of the Middle Ages. This was hardly outrageous — quite the contrary — but Donoso considered that certain points required clarification. He responded (on November 15, 1852) with a letter to the editor of the journal. This letter lacks the cohesion and style of the Fornari missive and is burdened with much of the overabundance of his early work, but it does contain some pertinent observations.

Donoso begins by crediting the Church with having created European civilization. In the midst of the chaos, corruption, and barbarism of the Middle Ages, he says, the Church effected "a second creation." But by no means does he wish to resuscitate the Middle Ages. He simply wants to restore those Christian principles which history has proved capable of constituting a social order. Much to its discredit, modernity has succeeded in distancing itself from Christian principles. But it has paid the penalty for its self-idolatry by being engulfed in the revolutionary tide.[36] He traces the genesis of the revolutionary ethos from the time when hereditary monarchy, reacting against the abuses of absolute monarchy, created parliamentarianism. Parliamentarianism divides sovereignty, denies its perpetuity, and destroys the intermediate bodies which restrict its scope. It is fated to have adverse effects on society because of its fatal ambiguity, which leads inexorably to either impotence or tyranny. Parliamentarianism denies the overarching law of unity with diver-

36. Donoso Cortés, "Carta al Director de la *Revue des deux mondes*" [November 15, 1852], *Obras,* vol. 2, pp. 765-67.

sity and constitutes the first stage in the development of the revolutionary spirit.[37]

De Broglie had proposed the alliance of Catholicism and freedom. Donoso can accept such an alliance as "the beautiful but rather bitter fruit of civilization."[38] But de Broglie goes on to equate modernity with freedom; and this, says Donoso, is a drastic mistake. Modernity is attempting to distort the intrinsic nature of things by joining together what should be kept separate — by refusing to choose between freedom and equality. It is attempting to better God's imperfect creation by opting for both. This is reflected, Donoso contends, in the precedence given to cleverness over character, and in the displacement of war from the battleground, where it strengthens, to the parliamentary rostrum, where it enfeebles. He again predicts the advent of a pagan and satanic demagogic power: looming on the horizon is a monolith which can be delayed, but not destroyed.[39]

Juan Donoso Cortés, Marqués de Valdegamas, Vizconde del Valle, died on the evening of May 3, 1853, an exemplary Christian death. After magnificent funeral rites, his body was interred in the crypt of the Church of St. Philippe du Roule. His remains were transferred to Madrid on May 11, 1900, along with those of Moratín, Meléndez Valdés, and Goya.[40] In one of those striking coincidences which justify history, the author of the "black prophecies" returned to Madrid together with the painter of the "black sketches." There he found his resting place, in the royal cemetery of San Isidro el Real.

Donoso, not unlike Nietzsche, believed that he spoke to people of the future. His friends and adversaries never quite understood him. He called the modern world hideous, and the modern world did not take it lightly. His defenders, such as Veuillot in France and Buss in Germany, were rough ultramontanes who never fathomed his thought. Donoso's impact on the age was made not through

37. "Carta al Director de la *Revue des deux mondes,*" pp. 769-70, 775.
38. "Carta al Director de la *Revue des deux mondes,*" p. 774.
39. "Carta al Director de la *Revue des deux mondes,*" pp. 776-78.
40. Schramm, p. 332.

complexity of thought, but through the golden brilliance of his oratory and the high drama of his prophecies. The rest soon fell into oblivion. As Schmitt notes, "A few years after 1848, Donoso Cortés was forgotten in Europe. His name had passed to join the list of the solitaires, ignored and silenced, of the nineteenth century."[41]

41. Schmitt, p. 70.

CHAPTER ELEVEN

Donoso as Cassandra

Donoso was obsessed by the overpowering force of evil in the world, a force he did not hesitate to call omnipotent. The fragility of humanity distressed him to the core. He probably exaggerated both. But he was childlike in his enthusiasm whenever he encountered a good man or a favorable turn of events, conscious as he was that historical gravity would soon claim another victim. Donoso has been called the Cassandra of the age. This is an apt description, as he scrutinized the future with eyes which were both prophetic and jaundiced. Together with most scholars who have considered this question, he did not believe himself to have been endowed with prophetic gifts. Yet it is precisely those predictions which culminated in his "black prophecies" that saved Donoso from the obscurity to which at one time he appeared to be irremediably condemned.

A skeptic might suggest, and not without reason, that Donoso had an irrepressible urge to prognosticate — an urge that amounted to a genuine compulsion. He made so many predictions that some of them were bound to come true. It was nearly impossible for him to analyze any social or political event without envisioning its future development and predicting its final outcome. Nevertheless, there are treasures to be found here. Donoso's predictions include the grotesque, the fanciful, and the simply outrageous. But surprising insights are also found — insights rendered all the more believable by the dramatic way in which they are presented. Whatever lapses there are into bad taste, pure fantasy, or illogic (and there are several), they are more than compensated for by these flashes of insight. As Donoso once stated in jest, he was "laughing at the fools while waiting for the deluge."[1]

When historical events appeared to be unintelligible, he would lift his eyes to God and read there what he otherwise could not understand.[2] He also believed in making effective use of sound reason, common sense, and everyday insight. In any case, he seldom made a prediction based solely on sustained argument or weighty consideration. I once observed that Donoso "possessed the unique if disconcerting talent of wrapping his practical insights — on target more often than not — with impressive but usually questionable theoretical justifications."[3] In effect, his speculative turns and theoretical constructions are used to provide an attractive facade for his insights. They constitute the cocoon from which the insight will emerge. Donoso took his predictions seriously, as he did most things. But strange to say, especially considering the seriousness of his physical maladies and his increasing morbidity, he was never really overwhelmed by them. Guizot was very perceptive when he called Donoso a good-humored Jeremiah.

Among the less apocalyptic prophecies, we find Donoso's accurate prediction of the participants and general locale of the Crimean War. There is also his envisioning of the Slavs and Germans as holding in their hands the future of Europe. Over a hundred years in advance, he predicted the disintegration of the British Empire and

---

1. Donoso Cortés, "Carta a Gabino Tejado" [September 16, 1851], *Obras Completas de Don Juan Donoso Cortés,* ed. Carlos Valverde (Madrid: BAC, 1970), vol. 2, p. 718.

2. Donoso Cortés, "Carta al Conde Raczynski" [December 7, 1851], *Obras,* vol. 2, p. 953.

3. R. A. Herrera, "Donoso Cortés: A Second Look at Political Apocalyptic," *Continuity* 11 (1987): 63-64.

warned of the infiltration of revolutionary ideology into the Catholic Church by means of semantic equivocation. Granted, such prophecies, surprising as they may seem, can easily be explained away as lucky guesses or fruits of deductive reasoning. More impressive, however, is Donoso's prediction that the union of socialism and Slavism would be a decisive event in world history — that revolution would break out in St. Petersburg before it would in London. This assuredly ranks as one of the most significant prophecies of the century. According to Donoso, such events would signal the "great hour" of Russia and the "great punishment" for Europe, which, in turn, would infect Russia with the disease which would cause its demise.

Donoso's long-term predictions speak of the veritable ocean of blood there will be once the revolutionary flood has engulfed the world. The age of the masses will be generated by a process combining galloping democratization, mechanization, and centralization: a process abetted by a multiplicity of new inventions, such as the telegraph. This process will destroy all intermediate bodies and leave the atomistic individual face to face with an all-powerful state. The outcome will be a type of socialism which will inevitably be taken to its radical extreme. Donoso suggests that liberal-socialist ideology has infiltrated the collective mind to the point of causing a distortion of fundamental verities. The result will be malevolent and pervasive hypocrisy. Tyranny, slavery, and worse degradations will be tolerated, even welcomed, if presented under the umbrella of humanitarianism, freedom, or any of the other shibboleths of the day. The shattering of the religious domain has already caused dangerous upheavals in the subsidiary realms of society and politics. Nothing can be more detestable than the degradation of Christianity. Kierkegaard speaks of a "frightful illusion." Donoso attempts to spell out the consequences of this frightful illusion on the social and political orders.

A simple account of Donoso's predictions is impressive, and made all the more so by the baroque style and highly charged language in which he packaged them. Donoso had a gift for conveying physical images of the advancing evil monolith: it is a gelatinous, noxious mass intent on destroying everything select and praiseworthy so as to reduce humanity to a faceless conglomerate of windowless atoms. Donoso's black prophecies are the prose equivalent of Goya's black sketches. Perhaps they are not so finely etched, but they are certainly as poignant and horrifying. Both Goya and Donoso realized that in times of intensified struggle, when people are numbed by horror, only the more shocking forms of communication — exaggeration, the bizarre phrase, the distorted image, the fragmented portrait — can awaken the sensitivity of desensitized minds.

It would be difficult enough not to sympathize with Donoso's outrage if one knew nothing of the man himself. But this was a very gentle man, a man given to small talk and raillery, delighting in good cigars and bonbons, vain to the point of wearing a small hairpiece. Donoso visited palaces and fashionable watering places, hovels of the poor, even jails. He was equally at home with aristocrats and the impoverished. During his last years, when he was living at the Spanish embassy in Paris, he wrote to his father about how ironic it was that the one-time all-powerful Manuel Godoy, the Prince of Peace, was dying in a third-floor flat of the Rue de la Michodière, while he himself was living in a palace.[4]

In his later years, Donoso lived in an extremely austere manner. The robes of the diplomat hid the chains of the penitent. Mute witnesses to these years are the hair shirt and barbed harness kept at Don Benito.[5] Following such like-minded personalities as Cardinal Cisneros and St. Francis Borgia, Donoso developed a spirituality very much in the Spanish tradition. Both pious and warlike, Spanish Christianity is ever engaged in the conquest of the City of Man while preparing an expedition to take heaven by storm. The Franciscan mystic Fray Juan de los Angeles exemplified this sensibility nicely in his work *Diálogos de la Conquista del Reino de Dios.*

---

4. Donoso Cortés, "Carta a su Padre" [October 10, 1851], *Obras,* vol. 2, p. 706.

5. John T. Graham, *Donoso Cortés: Utopian Romanticist and Political Realist* (Columbia: University of Missouri Press, 1974), p. 123 n. 47.

It must be admitted, however, that Dostoyevsky's Grand Inquisitor also belongs to this family, even if only in black-sheep fashion.

While Donoso came to understand thoroughly the liberal ideology which had captivated him as a youth, he was engaged in the additional task of coming to terms with his own Spanish heritage. When he realized that they were in conflict, he abandoned liberalism and struggled against it. He rose up to defend the tradition of the warrior priest, the tradition which had forged the heroic Spain of the Reconquista and the *Siglo de Oro*. Marcelino Menéndez Pelayo, that paradigmatic Spanish Catholic, notes that Donoso's vehement, apocalyptic eloquence numbers him among the disciples of Bonald and places him together with Pascal and Bishop Huet in the class of radical pessimists.[6] This is only a fairly safe generalization which requires much clarification. No doubt, Donoso was a radical. He met the radical ideology of the revolution with radical invective. He was, in fact, more of a throwback to the Granada wars than a pale imitation of Cassandra. But what he most valued was under attack and in danger of perishing. He had to struggle against those movements, forged by cultural philistines, which were causing the destruction of religion and allowing the natural gravity of fallen humanity to reassert itself.

It is Donoso's more spectacular predictions, those which merit the name of prophecy, which interest us today, living as we do at the end point of a negative historical spiral. The real hell under the attractive guise of the earthly paradise is no longer quiescent. Its horrors filter through the cracks in our fragile social and political structures while the majority of people gambol happily down the primrose path to destruction. In the past two centuries, the terrors of the French Revolution have been cosmetically repaired, the two great wars have been all but forgotten, and the death camps and gulags, apart from isolated cries of outrage, have been reduced to the status of tourist attractions. The oceans of blood predicted by

6. J. M. Sánchez de Muniain, ed., *Antología General de Menéndez Pelayo* (Madrid: BAC, 1956), vol. 1, nos. 1752-53.

Donoso have inundated the world, and the world remains insensitive — even though the depredations follow to a surprising degree the blueprint he traced well over a century ago.

What intrigued Donoso was not so much the individual event, no matter how important, but the struggle between conflicting forces, and the dragon's teeth sown by the combat. Following St. Augustine, he found the raison d'être of history in the struggle between the two cities or pyramids of loyalty, the City of Man and the City of God. But, as a minor Augustine, Donoso identified the City of God with the Catholic Church and the City of Man with revolution. Very much aware of the gravity of the struggle, he was even more pessimistic than the great African theologian.

The modern constitutional state triumphed together with deism, "a theology and metaphysics which banished the 'miracle,' the 'exception' in every form from the world," as Schmitt indicates.[7] The bourgeoisie, characterized by Donoso as "the discussing class," had substituted the word for the Word, the human word for the divine Logos. Because of this, its religion consisted, despite appearances to the contrary, in freedom of speech and freedom of the press. Nietzsche faulted Socrates for failure to understand that reason carries its *quantum* of passion. Donoso faulted the bourgeoisie for failure to understand that discussing, bartering, compromising, and incessant chattering constitute a betrayal of instinct as well as of responsibility. He was convinced that the march of dissolution beginning at the Reformation and leading to the French Revolution had continued with the revolutionary episodes of the nineteenth century and was still advancing. The atheo-democratic movement was in the ascendancy and had everywhere to go.

While Tocqueville, Niebuhr, Bruno Bauer, and others agreed with Donoso as to the inevitability of the democratization, mechanization, and centralization of humanity, they did not greet its coming with his extreme horror. In Donoso's vision, the joining of the

7. Carl Schmitt, *Political Theology,* trans. G. Schwab (Cambridge: MIT Press, 1985), p. 36.

axiom of the natural goodness of man with the deification of reason had created a behemoth which, feeding exclusively on the narcissistic contemplation of itself, would not accept any limitation. Religious, moral, and political barriers would be destroyed, and the bonds holding men together would be shattered. In banishing the exception, the "miracle," the bourgeoisie eliminated, among other things, the "miracle" in its political form — that is, dictatorship, the sole remedy in times of crisis. The only remaining nexus was appetite; the only organizing principle, sheer force.

Donoso's extremism was derived both from his personality and from his native soil. José Ortega y Gasset once referred to Spain as a Western Tibet[8] — a rather jaundiced commentary, but withal an appropriate way to convey the substratum of the alien and unique which subsists even today under the state-of-the-art facade of contemporary Spain. One recalls the astonishment of Hilaire Belloc upon hearing the Salve Regina sung in a small Spanish village: it was "harsh, full of battle and agony."[9] One thinks also of Unamuno's predilection for the "Spanish Christ": livid, squalid, bloody, and ferocious.[10] The notion of life as tragic spectacle, as combat, as the bullring writ large, was something taken for granted by Donoso.

The grand illusions and universal panaceas concocted in Donoso's day were not so different from those afflicting the contemporary world. They have in common that romanticizing of economics which leads, as Donoso said, to spiritual poverty and catastrophe. The specious advances of "freedom" — the destruction of institutions, the corruption of morals, and the disappearance of forms — portend that tyranny of gigantic proportions which Donoso feared and foretold. Yet despite the dreadfulness of the prognosis, his advocacy of dictatorship as a remedy for states of exception does imply

8. Cited by J. N. Hillgarth, *The Spanish Kingdoms of 1215-1516* (Oxford: Clarendon Press, 1978), vol. 2, p. 625 n. 3.

9. J. B. Morton, ed., *Hilaire Belloc: Selected Essays* (Baltimore: Penguin, 1958), pp. 82-83.

10. Miguel de Unamuno, *Mi Religión y otros ensayos* (Madrid: Espasa-Calpe, 1968), pp. 29, 33.

that at least provisional holding actions against this ultimate horror are possible. It further implies that there probably will exist at least a residue of civilization worth preserving well into the future. This is no small consolation. And Tassara's "new Middle Age" remains a hope, however distant.[11]

As Donoso learned from St. Augustine, everything that exists is ontologically good. It is good insofar as it is; that is, insofar as it manifests God's creative goodness. Evil is an absence of due good, an absence of being. Moral or social evil is a sort of paring away of being which prods the individual or society closer to chaos and nothingness. As Gilson has suggested, the principal target of revolutionary hubris is Being itself.[12] The creation of a new world demands the destruction of the actually existing world. Gilson may have had in mind the short distance separating Rousseau's *Confessions* from Nietzsche's *Beyond Good and Evil* and Freud's *Civilization and Its Discontents*. Rousseau initiated a radical transvaluation of values which accomplished, through his disciples, a violent break with the values, traditions, customs, and usages of the past. He was the first modern to resolutely reject the work of seventeen centuries and propose the destruction of the existing world so as to create a better world in his own image. In this he was followed by Nietzsche and, to a lesser degree, by Freud.

His illness and neurotic symptomatology notwithstanding, Donoso's predictions were more than a reflection of his always mercurial state of mind. His most somber predictions coincided with the preparations for the elaborate wedding of Napoleon III and Eugenia de Montijo. If any emotion can be said to have been long-lived, it was his fear of rootlessness, which fed his antirationalism and his deep, though grudging, love of his fatherland. This fear slowly divested him, to some extent, of his inflated intellectualism and the philosophical baggage he had acquired as a youth. The

11. Graham, pp. 178-84.
12. Etienne Gilson, "The Terrors of the Year Two Thousand," in *The Canadian Catholic Review* 2, no. 11 (December 1984): 23, 459.

Spaniard, the man from the land of the *conquistadores,* emerged with a vengeance. The change is manifested in the violence of his oratory, the florid exaggeration of his prose, the surgical deftness of his diplomacy, and the blackness of his prophecies.

It has been stated that Donoso's most terrifying prophecies were proved right, at least in part, by the emergence of Lenin and Hitler. It might be added that his analysis of the coming behemoth already envisions the constitution of that anomic, deracinated mass so expertly analyzed by Ortega in his *Revolt of the Masses,* and that it can be applied even today to the clear and present danger presented by those that Viereck calls "the underground barbarian of our urban jungles."[13] In such an analysis, the French Revolution becomes a mere "type" of things to come. The abominations of the contemporary world are simply links on the same chain, the unpacking of a Pandora's box opened several centuries ago.

The most notorious and important of Donoso's predictions was that of the eventual triumph of socialism and the constitution of a vast Slavic world state under the aegis of Russia, which would itself be destroyed by contamination from its conquered foe. To predict an eventual symbiosis of socialism and Slavic nationalism which would resurrect the aspirations of Peter the Great's "Third Rome" was a considerable feat. It is all the more impressive in light of the fact that the majority view (and his own) at the time was that tsarist Russia was the major bulwark of conservatism, if not reaction, in Europe. An argument can also be made that the triumph of egalitarianism, the tilt toward socialism in Europe and America, and the vaunted collapse of the Soviet Union correspond to the general lines of Donoso's speculations. But this argument is both forced and trivial. A long look at our own society — fragmented, clustered in tribal units, coerced from above and below, condemned to the biblical confusion of tongues — cannot help but elicit admiration for this man who may have been graced with a glimpse into the future.

13. Peter Viereck, *Conservatism Revisited* (New York: Charles Scribner's Sons, 1950), p. 31.

The original Cassandra, daughter of Priam and Hecuba, beloved of Apollo, had a rather checkered career. According to the legend, Apollo bestowed on her the spirit of prophecy, on the understanding that she would accept his advances. But she did not, and Apollo revenged himself by ordaining that her prophecies should never be believed. Later ravaged by Ajax, she became the booty of Agamemnon and was murdered together with him. Donoso had a less bloody but equally tragic fate. He died a young man ravaged by a dreadfully painful and perhaps extremely humiliating disease. His meteoric rise to fame was soon forgotten, his thought dismissed from serious consideration (except, perhaps, in times of peril) and doomed to become, at best, a minor enclave of research for the scholar, a suggestive oddity for the politician, an intramural academic sport. His prophecies, however, are still with us: dusty antiques which, given attentive consideration, prove to possess strange and marvelous powers of enchantment.

CHAPTER TWELVE

Epilogue

Donoso's propheticism having been considered, an attempt should now be made to determine the extent of his contribution to political thought. It is of particular importance to dispel the canard that he was no more than an atavistic throwback to the worst of the Middle Ages, a man lusting to rekindle the fires of the Inquisition. What renders the charge at all plausible is that he did aspire to revive those principles which made the best of the Middle Ages possible. And the tone of his thought is, to a great extent, medieval and juristic. He uses many terms borrowed from theology, as well as analogies taken from religion and theology.

Schmitt is not off the mark in stressing Donoso's "metaphysical consciousness" and "decisionism,"[1] although his own thought is best described as what Willms calls "political realism," while Donoso's would be a variety of "political fictionalism."[2] Donoso was

---

1. Carl Schmitt, *Political Theology*, trans. G. Schwab (Cambridge: MIT Press, 1985), pp. 51, 53-54; Schmitt, *Interpretación Europea de Donoso Cortés* (Madrid: Rialp, 1963), pp. 73-74.

2. Willms, "Politics as Politics: Carl Schmitt's 'Concept of the Political' and the Tradition of European Political Thought," *History of European Ideas,* vol. 13, no. 4, pp. 371-72. Willms distinguishes "political fictionalism," which subordinates politics to higher principles or truths, from "political realism," which is the

influenced by many thinkers and many currents of thought, all of which intertwine so tightly that it is difficult to determine to which he was most indebted. Schramm, for example, lists Rousseau, Constant, Royer-Collard, Guizot, Chateaubriand, Lista, and de Maistre.[3] In a pamphlet written some sixteen years after *Donoso Cortés, su Vida y su Pensamiento,* Schramm emphasizes the influence of the French traditionalists, citing several points of contact. Both Bonald and Donoso believe that political ideology is conditioned by religion and that religious and political concepts are analogous. Donoso's notion of "Christian civilization" approximates Bonald's notion of "Christian society." De Maistre's deduction of the state from the presence of evil in man and his notion of "le combat à outrance du christianisme et du philosophisme" has analogues in Donoso's thought, albeit found in rather different contexts.[4]

A lengthy catalogue of possible influences is provided by Graham — too lengthy to reproduce — but he seems to settle on Saint-Simon, Comte, Vico, Bossuet, and St. Augustine as the major sources.[5] He adds, perceptively, that Donoso did not borrow from any one thinker or school, but assimilated from the whole spectrum.[6] Fr. Valverde marks the prime importance of St. Augustine and his "metaphysics of order," which he sees reflected in many important aspects of Donoso's thought.[7] Although Valverde minimizes the

---

constantly repeated attempt to conceive of politics as what in fact it is. The distinction is both convenient and self-serving. "Political fictionalism" includes all theologically derived politics; "political realism" includes such thinkers as Ockham, Machiavelli, and Hobbes.

3. Edmund Schramm, *Donoso Cortés, su Vida y su Pensamiento,* trans. Ramón de la Serna (Madrid: Espasa-Calpe, 1936), pp. 49, 50, 60, 69, 82-83, 112, and 144-45.

4. Schramm, *Donoso Cortés, Ejemplo del Pensamiento de la Tradición* (Madrid: Ateneo, 1952), pp. 37-41.

5. John T. Graham, *Donoso Cortés: Utopian Romanticist and Political Reformer* (Columbia: University of Missouri Press, 1974), pp. 36, 93, 97, and 101-2.

6. Graham, p. 93.

7. *Obras Completas de Don Juan Donoso Cortés,* ed. Carlos Valverde (Madrid: BAC, 1970), vol. 1, pp. 109-10.

importance of Vico, who was probably known to Donoso through Michelet, he cites Hegel as a possible influence.[8] As Juretschke had previously noted, however, Donoso's Hegelian terminology came from his reading of Guizot and Cousin, and so this source should not be overemphasized.[9]

This lack of unanimity, which reflects so well the vagaries of scholarly judgment, stems in large part from the fact that scholars tend to read Donoso as if he himself had been primarily a scholar. He was not. Donoso was a man of vast but patchy erudition; he was an encyclopedic but hardly discriminating reader. His style, intelligence, and prophetic élan were of a different order. He was a statesman, a courtier, a politician, a journalist, an exceptional orator, always on better terms with the spoken than the written word. As a writer he would fall someplace between the elegant gentility of a Cardinal Newman and the tasteless but vigorous style of a Leon Bloy. He was indebted to many: to St. Augustine, the French traditionalists, Saint-Simon, Fray Luis de Granada, even to Proudhon. Scripture is a pervasive influence. But these borrowings suffer a drastic sea change once they are appropriated by Donoso and inserted, at times fancifully and arbitrarily, into the network of his own interests and concerns. Donoso is something of a literary Melchizedek.

The most important event of the epoch was, of course, the French Revolution. Donoso was born and lived under its shadow. Even today, the French Revolution is considered by many to have been the splendid *novum* which brought about the rebirth of France and put humanity on the path to a future of unparalleled greatness. It destroyed the *ancien régime* grounded on privilege and prejudice and replaced it with a superior new order based on reason and equity. The French Revolution was the watershed out of which the majority of modern political institutions emerged, the point of departure for those humanitarian and egalitarian reforms which are the boast of contemporary man.

8. *Obras,* vol. 1, p. 110.
9. *Obras,* vol. 1, p. 111 n. 43.

Donoso was a voice of opposition, closer to Burke and de Maistre than to any of the apologists of revolution. A convert of sorts, he turned from his early liberalism to a conservative, near-reactionary position. Even in his youth, however, he would have agreed with these remarks Burke made in a letter written in March 1790:

> I confess to you that I have no great opinion of that sublime abstract, metaphysic reversionary, contingent humanity which in *cold blood* can subject the *present time,* and those whom we *daily see and converse with,* to *immediate* calamities in favor of the future and uncertain benefit of persons who *only exist in idea.*[10]

Donoso understood society as being the product of the lengthy and unconscious effort of generations, the magnificent though fragile growth of centuries. Any rationalistic tampering might set loose the beast in man and end in disaster.

Donoso cannot be understood other than as a man of faith. It was his religious faith which kept him from losing hope in humanity. Schmitt finds his contempt for humanity so pronounced that it was not even romantically interesting or attractive.[11] But Schmitt seems to forget that Donoso, even to the end, affirmed the grandeur of man. Granted, he did this only in spite of himself, simply because it was taught by the Church. In so doing, however, he provided a nice contrast to those revolutionary enthusiasts who were so persuaded of the grandeur of man that they did away with God in order to clear the decks of competition.

Donoso's attacks on the middle class, parliamentarianism, and discussion were valiant efforts to save humanity from its lower belly — efforts made in an attempt to prevent the coming of a debased humanity, an endlessly chattering mass, fathered by the romantic illusion of eternal dialogue. His transition from defending legiti-

10. Harvey C. Mansfield, Jr., ed., *Selected Letters of Edmund Burke* (Chicago: University of Chicago Press, 1984), p. 284.

11. Schmitt, *Interpretación,* p. 125.

macy to advocating dictatorship parallels his disenchantment with discussion and his rejection of the principle of intelligence. Donoso came to realize that, in the tradition of the Psalms, God had withdrawn and left a vacuum which malevolent forces were attempting to fill.

Hans Jonas has pointed out that the opposite of the biblical view of God is not atheism, which contemplates a neutral world, but paganism, which deifies the world.[12] The majority of the new gospels which inspired the French Revolution and which were generated by it could be categorized as neopagan. They proposed a liberation from the past, a surgical detachment from those bonds of tradition which make the future a real possibility. Donoso saw that these revolutionary ideologies, when developed in history, would ultimately separate humanity from the objective worlds of being and inherited civilization, fragmenting it into a multiplicity of random atoms. This would be the culmination of a process which began with the weakening of the notion of God and which would end with its disappearance: speaking existentially, the death of God.

Donoso has been criticized for his pessimism, for his radicalization of the doctrine of original sin. However, inasmuch as he was attacking ideologies based on the axiom of the naturally good man, he was to some extent justified in his pessimism. He was engaged in war, not academic debate. The horror and dread with which he viewed revolution account for much of the extremism of his attack and the exaggeration of his language. One of Donoso's merits is that he raised a cry against the optimism of the age and attacked its basis in the natural goodness of man. He made it clear that this notion was not only a theological absurdity but also a social pollutant, in that it justified in principle the full spectrum of human activity, including its most base and vicious manifestations.

His defense of dictatorship for states of exception is noteworthy, especially since Donoso envisioned the future as a nearly uninter-

12. Hans Jonas, *The Phenomenon of Life* (New York: Delta, 1968), p. 249.

rupted state of exception. The idea of dictatorship as a provisional holding action provides a scintilla of hope in an otherwise bleak scenario, as it seems to imply that the residue of civilization still pulsating within society will not be immediately destroyed, but will be subjected to a lengthy siege. As an antidote to revolutionary tyranny, the "dictatorship of the saber" presents a solution for the danger at hand and keeps ultimate chaos at a distance. The violence of his invective in discussing this point has not served to endear Donoso to future generations. He has been attacked as a precursor of fascism and Nazism — a charge which gained credence when his work began attracting the attention of scholars (such as Carl Schmitt) with antidemocratic views and National Socialist connections, if not sympathies. As early as 1950, for example, only a few years after the end of World War II and hardly a time of German prosperity, a luxury edition of Donoso's collected works was published at Cologne under the editorship of Albert Maier.[13]

Donoso realized that literature is a reflection of the society which produces it. From the time of his articles in *El Correo Nacional* (1838), he was aware of the importance of romanticism in the revolutionary struggle against the past and existing social conditions. He never tired of emphasizing the priority of ideas over political action, their role as the moving cause of social change. Donoso anticipated Nietzsche's critique of Socrates in *The Birth of Tragedy* when he suggested that rationalism dries up those inner springs of life which have the power of mobilizing society. Accordingly, he repudiated the claims of reason. As far as he was concerned, reason had renounced its legitimate authority by rejecting God and was being punished for its pride by being forced to worship its own creation, the Absurd.

Donoso was able to probe further in his analysis of autonomous man than most of his conservative peers precisely because of his theological tilt. He could see the truth: the more autonomy man aspires to, the lesser he becomes; the further he strays from God, the

---

13. Albert Maier, ed., *Donoso Cortés: Briefe, parlamentarische Reden und diplomatische Berichte aus den letzten Jahren seines Lebens (1809-1853)* (Köln, 1950).

more inhuman. Schmitt exaggerates, or misreads in the light of his own concerns, a truly important insight when he declares that "the phrases of Donoso palpitate with the understanding that the absolute man makes the superman necessary . . . and [that] the superman brings as his dialectical twin brother . . . the infrahuman."[14] But if this statement is understood to mean that a humankind separated from God will generate tyrannies in which the rulers and the ruled, subject to no limitation and mediated by sheer power, will come to face each other as master and slave, it can be accepted as an accurate rendering of Donoso's thought.

One of the most valuable insights found in Donoso's works, one shared by other perceptive thinkers as well, is that the cause of the radical violence of the social and political upheavals in the modern world is the Christian spirit which revolution appropriates in a ghastly, distorted form. Revolution is the malevolent doppelgänger of Christianity which, when joined to rationalism and the idealism of abstract quantity, creates a public orthodoxy as inflexible as it is ubiquitous. The abstract ideal must be served at all costs. Donoso opposes this tyranny by attacking the notion of progress and thus rejecting the liberal interpretation of the historical meaning of the century. There is no ascending movement, but there is a descending movement; no paradise at the end of the road, but a real hell.

The liberation of the family from patriarchal tyranny has led to the destruction of the family; liberation from punitive law, to massive crime; the abolition of capital punishment, to killing *en masse*. The transfer of war from the physical to the spiritual domain has brought drastic and terrible consequences. The malevolent double of Christianity will attempt to destroy all normative values of traditional society, wherever they are found, by submerging them in the dissolvent of radical democratic ideology. This liberation from limitation, tradition, custom, and law — that is to say, from civilization — prepares the way for the coming of the "last man," the "trousered ape," "mass man" and his comrades-in-arms.

14. Schmitt, *Interpretación,* pp. 67-68.

A horror loomed on the horizon, but it could not be identified with any of its specific manifestations. When Donoso spoke of a conjunction between Russian imperialism and socialism, this was an educated guess, however brilliant. Much was left unsaid. The horror was and is protean, not unlike the apocalyptic seven-headed dragon which captivated the medieval imagination. Rampaging egalitarianism and its sequelae can be found in the least likely places. When both internal and external resistance, conscience and force have been obviated, then society awaits the exterminating angel.

Especially relevant today is Donoso's attack on the media. He was a journalist, if something of a gifted amateur. But in his opinion, the press was one of the most effective agents of mechanization and centralization. It was the facade behind which the powers-that-be attempted to impose a despotism under the unctuous guise of pedagogical humanism. The press turned questions of life and death into mere issues and then disposed of them by talking them to death. Empty prose analogous to the vacuous chatter of the brothel became the norm. Eternal verities were given equal status with trivia, and principles were transmuted into mere preferences subject to individual caprice. Journalism was becoming a civic priesthood which would erode human dignity by stealth, encouraging idle chatter and promoting a universal relativism which would prove far worse than ignorance.

Donoso's speculations have been savaged by his enemies and faulted by his admirers. Neither Lord Acton nor Ortega thought highly of his work. Marx was surprised that Herzen would take the trouble to criticize him. Even Schmitt declares his style antiquated, his method in disuse, his arguments otiose and partially contradicted by history.[15] Schramm scores his pessimism, his belief in the total depravity of humankind, his nebulous conception of Catholic civilization, and his belief in the necessary triumph of evil in the world.[16] More can be said. His theoretical turns are often lacking in precision. He is sometimes out of his depth, as when he discusses Hegel or

15. Schmitt, *Interpretación,* p. 131.
16. Schramm, *Donoso Cortés, Ejemplo . . . ,* pp. 34-35.

Kant. Although he understood philosophical method as reasoning from individual facts to underlying principles,[17] he often used it in a cavalier fashion, forcing his material into the procrustean bed required by the argument at hand. The vigor and élan of the three great discourses and the letter to Cardinal Fornari tower above most of his other writings. We find in the *Ensayo* fine passages, impressive images, and acute insights which are lost in an ocean of precious, at times heavy-handed theological speculation. His terms are often imprecise. A good example is that of "philosophical civilization," which seems to have been a convenient umbrella under which Donoso could place whatever he considered opposed to Christianity.

Despite the criticisms of friend and foe, however, much of great value remains. Schmitt believes that Donoso should be recognized as one of the greatest political thinkers of the nineteenth century because of his genial intuitions.[18] Schramm believes him to have been one of the greatest defenders of the European Christian tradition.[19] Suárez notes his amazing prescience regarding the direction in which the world is moving.[20] Graham considers him the first Christian positivist.[21] According to Viereck, he was in some ways the subtlest intellect in the entire history of conservatism.[22] On the historical level, his influence is reflected in Pius IX's *Syllabus Errorum,* Franco's Organic Law of 1967, and his constant, at times disturbing, presence in conservative polemics. For example, Cánovas del Castillo, in 1869, used arguments similar to those of Donoso to oppose universal suffrage.[23]

17. Donoso Cortés, "Filosofía de la Historia: Juan Bautista Vico," *Obras,* vol. 1, pp. 619-20.

18. Schmitt, *Interpretación,* p. 131.

19. Schramm, *Donoso Cortés, Ejemplo . . . ,* p. 43.

20. Federico Suárez Verdeguer, *Introducción a Donoso Cortés* (Madrid: Rialp, 1964), p. 143.

21. Graham, p. 1.

22. Peter Viereck, *Conservatism: From John Adams to Churchill* (Princeton: D. Van Nostrand, 1956), p. 63.

23. Ramón Menéndez Pidal, *Historia de España,* vol. 34: *La Era Isabelina y el Sexenio Democrático* [1834-1874] (Madrid: Espasa-Calpe, 1981), p. 656.

Whatever his deficiencies, Donoso is truly unique, both as an interpreter of his age and as an unsettling presence who puts many of the cherished institutions of the modern world under attack, scoring their negligible philosophical and moral underpinnings and pointing to their tainted origin. He prods contemporary man to rethink his principles and retrace his steps. The gigantic despotism which he predicted would arrive under the deceptive guise of a beneficent humanism cannot be dismissed out of hand. Perhaps this gentle man, very possibly a saint, who was obsessed by the ubiquity of evil and the nothingness of man, was graced by Providence with the task of imparting an admonition to the world that the world was loath to hear. Perhaps we should apply to Donoso the words of Russell Kirk:

> If a conservative order is indeed to return, we ought to know the tradition which is attached to it, so that we may rebuild society; if it is not to be restored, still we ought to understand conservative ideas so that we may rake from the ashes what scorched fragments of civilization escape the conflagration of unchecked will and appetite.[24]

24. Russell Kirk, *The Conservative Mind* (South Bend: Gateway Editions, 1978), p. 10.

Selected Bibliography

I. Original Sources

Juan Donoso Cortés: Artículos Políticos en "El Piloto" [1837]. Introduction by Federico Suárez. Pamplona: EUNSA, 1992.

Juan Donoso Cortés: Artículos Políticos en "El Piloto" [1839-1840]. Introduction by Federico Suárez. Pamplona: EUNSA, 1992.

Obras Completas de Don Juan Donoso Cortés. Edited by Juan Juretschke. 2 vols. Madrid: BAC, 1946.

Obras Completas de Don Juan Donoso Cortés. Edited by Carlos Valverde. 2 vols. Madrid: BAC, 1970.

II. English Translations

Catholicism, Liberalism, and Socialism. [*Ensayo sobre el Catolicismo, el Liberalismo y el Socialismo.*] Translated by M. V. Goddard. Albany: Preserving Christian Publications, 1989.

A Defense of Representative Government. [*Lecciones de Derecho Político*]. Translated by Vincent McNamara. North York: Captus Press, 1991.

"Speech on Dictatorship." In Bela Menczer, *Catholic Political Thought, 1789-1848.* London: Burns Oats, 1952.

III. Books on Donoso

Chaix-Ruy, Jules. *Donoso Cortés, théologien de l'histoire et prophète.* Paris: Beauchesne, 1956.

Copeland, Raymond F. *Donoso Cortés and His Social Thought.* Ph.D. dissertation. St. Louis: St. Louis University, 1950.

Elías de Tejada, Francisco. *Para una interpretación extremena de Donoso Cortés.* Caceres, 1949.

Graham, John T. *Donoso Cortés: Utopian Romanticist and Political Realist.* Columbia: University of Missouri Press, 1974.

Kennedy, John J. *Donoso Cortés as a Servant of the State.* Ph.D. dissertation. New York: Columbia University, 1954.

Manion, Christopher. *The Philosophy of History of Juan Donoso Cortés.* Ph.D. dissertation. Notre Dame: University of Notre Dame, 1985.

Sánchez Abelenda, Raul. *La teoría del poder en el pensamiento político de Juan Donoso Cortés.* Buenos Aires: EUDBA, 1969.

Schmitt, Carl. *Interpretación Europea de Donoso Cortés.* Introduction and prologue by Angel López-Amo. Madrid: Rialp, 1963.

————. *Political Romanticism.* Translated by Guy Oakes. Cambridge: MIT Press, 1986.

————. *Political Theology.* Translated by G. Schwab. Cambridge: MIT Press, 1985.

Schramm, Edmund. *Donoso Cortés, Ejemplo del pensamiento de la tradición.* Madrid: Ateneo, 1952.

————. *Donoso Cortés, su Vida y su Pensamiento.* Translated by Ramón de la Serna. Madrid: Espasa-Calpe, 1936.

Suárez Verdeguer, Federico. *Introducción a Donoso Cortés.* Madrid: Rialp, 1964.

Viereck, Peter. *Conservatism: From John Adams to Churchill.* Princeton: D. Van Nostrand, 1956.

————. *Conservatism Revisited*. New York: Charles Scribner's Sons, 1950.

Westemeyer, Dietmar. *Donoso Cortés, hombre de estado y teólogo*. Translated by J. S. Mazpule. Madrid: Editora Nacional, 1957.

Worden, Mark. *The Political Theory of Juan Donoso Cortés*. Ph.D. dissertation. Chicago: University of Chicago, 1966.

IV. Articles on Donoso

Araquistáin, Luis de. "Donoso Cortés y su resonancia en Europa." *Cuadernos*, no. 3 (September-December 1953).

Barth, Hans. "Juan Donoso Cortés und Giambattista Vico." *Hortulus Amicorum*. Zurich, 1949.

Brophy, Leo. "Donoso Cortés: Statesman and Apologist." *Irish Monthly* 78 (September 1950).

Brownson, Orestes A. "Church and State." *Catholic World* 5 (April 1867).

————. "Rights and Duties." *Brownson's Review* (October 1852).

Calvo Serer, Rafael. "Europa en 1949: Commentario a dos discursos de Donoso Cortés." *Arbor* (March 1949).

Carvajal, Rodrigo Fernández. "Los Constantes de Donoso Cortés." *Revista de estudios políticos* (1957).

Ceñal, Ramón. "La Filosofía de historia de Donoso Cortés." *Revista de filosofía* 40 (August 11, 1952).

————. "Vico and Nineteenth-Century Spanish Thought." *Giambattista Vico, An International Symposium*. Baltimore: Johns Hopkins Press, 1969.

Costa, Joaquín. "Filosofía política de Donoso Cortés." *Estudios Jurídicos y Políticos*. Madrid: Biblioteca Jurídica de Autores Españoles, T. 14 (1884).

Galindo Herrero, Santiago. "Donoso Cortés en la última etapa de su vida." *Arbor* 25 (May 1953).

Herrera, R. A. "Donoso Cortés: A Second Look at Political Apocalyptic." *Continuity*, no. 11 (1987).

————. "The Great in the Small: Donoso Cortés' Variation on a Theme from the *Civitas Dei*." *Augustiniana,* fascicles 1-4, 1988.

Menczer, Bela. "A Prophet of Europe's Disasters." *The Month* 183 (May 1947).

————. "Metternich and Donoso Cortés: Christian and Conservative Thought in the European Revolution." *Dublin Review* 201 (last quarter, 1948).

Neill, Thomas P. "Juan Donoso Cortés: Prophet of Our Time." *Catholic World* 170 (November 1949).

Przwara, Erich. "Donoso Cortés und das Heroische." *Das Buch der Zeit,* Zurich (September 1936).

Schramm, Edmund. "Der Junge Donoso Cortés (1809-1836)." *Spanische Forchungen der Corresgesellschaft.* Münster, 1933.

Suárez Verdeguer, Federico. "La primera posición política de Donoso Cortés." *Arbor* 16 (July-August 1946).

Valverde, Carlos. "Introducción." *Obras Completas de Juan Donoso Cortés,* vol. 1. Madrid: BAC, 1970.

Wilhelmsen, Frederick D. "Donoso Cortés and the Problem of Political Power." *Intercollegiate Review,* January-February 1967.

Index of Names